Sustainability –
A Guide for
Boards and C-Suites

Gilbert S. Hedstrom

ISBN: 1548322822
ISBN-13: 9781548322823

Contents

Preface

Gib Hedstrom

Sustainability has become a critical board-level issue that affects not only the work of directors, but also the work of the C-suite executives who report to them. The core business challenge has come into sharp focus. *How can we succeed without consuming too many resources or having a negative societal impact?* Working across the value chain, that challenge requires corporate leaders to:

- Create profitable, growing companies that approach zero (negative) and even net-positive environmental and social footprints; and
- Help suppliers and customers to do the same.

Over the next decade, we can expect environmental, social, and governance (ESG) factors increasingly to impact how companies choose: new businesses to buy, old businesses to reshape or shed, new offerings to create, and suppliers with which to partner.

Board members and C-suite executives own the sustainability agenda. Yet they continue to struggle with sustainability. I know that from first-hand experience. Over the years, I have been fortunate to meet with Fortune 500 boards and their committees on over 60 occasions – across about 20 companies and many industries. Roughly half of the meetings have been with a full board of directors, while the other meetings have been with a board committee. Typically, I am in the boardroom for an hour or two. Often I meet alone with the outside directors in "executive session" (after the CEO and other company executives leave the room).

In every one of the 60 meetings, the board members have asked some version of a single question regarding sustainability: *"How do we stack up?"* They want to understand: *Where does our company stand today vis-à-vis sustainability as compared with competitors, peers, and best practices? What are our biggest gaps? What actions should we take now?*

To help C-suite executives (and those advising the CEO) answer those questions, I developed the Corporate Sustainability Scorecard ™ C-suite rating system. Since the late 1990s, Hedstrom Associates and partners have used the Corporate Sustainability Scorecard with dozens of global corporations. In 2015, we ran a pilot program with 25 blue chip companies. The executives used the Scorecard and offered ideas to shape and refine it. Based on their input, we have updated the Scorecard and are now making it available to a broader corporate audience.

Sustainability – A Guide for Boards and C-Suites places the entire sustainability conversation in a simple, board-friendly context. Think of it as a "balanced scorecard" that executives and board members can use to engage in the "right" high-value strategic conversations about sustainability and business growth.

Introduction:
Navigating the Sustainability Transformation

On the Threshold of Transformation

These are such extraordinary times. We can expect unprecedented business and societal change over the coming decade. Across the globe, the rapidly expanding middle class is crashing into the fixed supply of natural resources to support that growth. Between 2015 and 2030, the size of the middle class globally will double,[1] which will result in exploding demand for consumer goods and resources. Already today, the natural systems that provide resources are strained severely.[2] Something has to give. And with change comes business opportunity as companies navigate the sustainability transformation.[3]

The last time society experienced such dramatic change was about 150 years ago. In a 20-year span from 1859 to 1879: oil was discovered in Titusville, PA (1859); the French engineer, J. J. Étienne Lenoir, invented the internal combustion engine (1859); and Thomas Edison invented the electric light bulb (1879). The inventions over those two decades unfolded years later as the industrial revolution of the late 1800s. Yet, in many ways, very little has changed since then. Consider that today we continue to drive oil-fueled vehicles, rely more than ever on light bulbs, and still burn little black rocks to keep our cell phones and iPads running.

Market forces, societal trends, and resource constraints are converging for the first time in history. However, with globalization, the digital transformation, and demands for greater transparency, these changes take place today far

3

more rapidly than the transformation during the late 19th and early 20th centuries. The entire global economic system is built on a set of assumptions that are eroding in front of our eyes. The century-old model of the industrial era is being shattered – not only by *Airbnb, Lyft*, and *Amazon*, but also by more traditional companies such as *GE, Philips, Unilever*, and dozens of other leading companies.

Such *massive and messy transformation* is changing every industry. Over the next decade, society can expect to see trillions of dollars in value created and destroyed. Markets are driving disruptive change. Two years ago, *Ford* CEO Mark Fields aggressively pursued a sustainability agenda: dramatically "light-weighting" the company's profitable product (F-150 trucks) by shifting from steel to aluminum. Fields launched the company on a "dual track" of sustainable mobility coupled with the traditional selling of vehicles. Yet, in 2017 he was replaced with a new CEO charged with moving even *faster* into sustainable mobility. Incremental improvements are yesterday's solution.

The Drivers: Economics 101

In a nutshell, here is the *problem – and opportunity*:

N.B. Human society has bumped up against the limits of economic and natural systems. Modern industrialism developed in a world far different from the one we live in today: people were few, while natural resources were plentiful. What emerged was a highly productive, take-make-waste system. Take resources out of the earth; make stuff; and throw it away. That system worked for a long time.

4

Not anymore. The current model is simply *not sustainable;* that is, not able to be maintained at a certain rate or level, and not able to be upheld or defended. The basic laws of supply and demand will wreak havoc for many companies while presenting significant opportunities for others. This transformation largely will transpire between now and 2030, driven by the economics of "supply and demand" (as Figure 1 illustrates).

Figure 1: Growing Demand

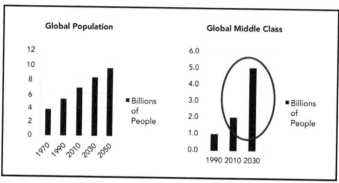

Source: Created from data produced by United Nations, Population Division

- *Demand:* From 2015 to 2030, the global middle class will double in size from 2.5 billion to about 5 billion.[4] Stop and think about that – particularly if you have spent time in Beijing, Shanghai, or Mexico City. Unless things change dramatically, the demand will double for food, cars, soda, diapers, and other "stuff" that today is purchased and discarded.

- *Supply:* Every company and industry requires a baseload supply of a stable physical environment within which to operate. Yet, to support this rapidly growing middle class demand, with a fixed amount of land, forest cover, fresh water, and other non-renewable resources on the planet, the environmental stability is dwindling quickly.[5]

- *Prices:* What happens when demand grows while supply is fixed or declining? Prices increase (at least in the absence of other market forces, such as tax incentives). Unfortunately, the powerful forces of supply and demand have been constrained by inadequate market pricing signals, especially related to carbon. Leading companies manage this situation by placing an internal price on carbon. A study by CDP (formerly Carbon Disclosure Project) noted that in 2016, 517 companies were using internal carbon pricing as an accounting and risk management tool (19% increase from 2015), and an additional 732 companies planned to implement one by 2018 (26% increase from 2015).[6]

With the supply and demand curves converging, the world is on the cusp of a resource revolution. This new industrial revolution will enable strong economic growth at an environmental "cost" (in terms of externalities such as pollution, CO_2 emissions, etc.) *far lower* than in the past. *Realistically, achieving high-productivity economic growth to support the 2.5 billion new members of the middle class presents the largest wealth-creation opportunity since the dawn of the industrial revolution.*[7]

Sustainability = Transformation

Sustainability is about transformation: creating profitable, growing companies that approach zero/negative and even net-positive environmental and social footprints, and that help their suppliers and customers to do the same. The transformation is under way. This is not tomorrow's opportunity. The signals of change are all around us today. For example:

- *Airbnb,* launched in 2008 and operating in 192 countries, appears on track to become the world's largest hotel chain without owning a single room – disrupting the entire industry.

- *Tesla* sold about 0.5 percent as many vehicles as General Motors did in 2015 (50,580 for Tesla compared with 9.8 million by General Motors). Yet, Tesla's market capitalization in June 2017 was ~$61 billion (as compared with General Motors at ~$52 billion).

- *Google* has invested a billion dollars in renewable energies and purchased the high-altitude, solar-powered drone maker Titan Aerospace. Google bought the satellite startup Skybox Imaging to help provide internet access to millions of people globally while also addressing social disruption (including disaster relief) and environmental damage.

- *Novelis,* a world leader in rolled aluminum products, has shifted its business model from a traditional linear one-way production model to a closed-loop model in which materials are reused rather than discharged as waste. The company is on track to achieve 80 percent recycled inputs by 2020, an increase from 33 percent in 2011.

- Digital ridesharing platforms such as *Uber* and *Lyft* have cut into the car rental and taxi market dramatically. Their dispatch model can increase utilization of an automobile up to five to eight times more than is typical with consumer-owned vehicles, thus enabling more efficient use of labor and capital resources through the use of information technology.

- *Unilever,* many years into its Sustainable Living Plan, aims to double the size of its business, while cutting in half the environmental impacts (footprint) of its products across the full value chain.

- *Waste Management* is a decade into transforming from its old economy business (hauling trash) to its new economy business (providing waste services).

Of note: simply because a company transforms itself to align with sustainability principles does not mean the driving force behind a newer start-up company or the transformation of an established one has much to do with sustainability. In the examples above, some companies (e.g., *Unilever* and *Novelis*) were driven heavily by sustainability principles, while others (e.g., *Airbnb, Lyft, Uber*) had relatively little to do with climate change, resource constraints or ESG issues.

In addition to the companies mentioned above, long-time companies like *BMW, DSM, DuPont, Marks and Spencer, Desso, Michelin,* and *Total* are busy shedding their "old economy" businesses to create tomorrow's growth businesses. In contrast, companies that cling to the "old economy" core businesses face significant pressures. In a historic (and surprise) vote on May 31, 2017, ExxonMobil's shareholders voted *for* a resolution (*against* Exxon's management) to report clearly how climate change impacts Exxon's business. *Investors are demanding that companies disclose the likely impact of global warming. Climate change is becoming the defining issue of our day.*

In its 2017 report on shareholder resolutions, The Conference Board notes that shareholder resolutions on ESG (environmental, social, and governance) issues now represent more than 43 percent of all voted resolutions, up from 34 percent in 2013. Shareholder proposals asking companies to disclose the business risks related to climate change continue to gain significant momentum. In 2017, 18 proposals on climate risk disclosure were brought to a vote, up from 13 in 2015. These proposals have now reached historically high levels of support: an average support of 39.2 percent of votes cast in 2017, up from 16.7 percent in 2015.[8]

As Table 1 illustrates, *virtually every industry is undergoing transformation*:

- *From* yesterday's *linear economy* focus where long-term growth has been more or less tied directly to growth in resource consumption across the full supply chain...

- *To* tomorrow's *circular economy* focus where growth in sales and profitability is decoupled from growth in resource consumption.[9] In the circular economy, resources remain in use for as long as possible; and at the end of a product's useful life, materials are recycled, reused, or regenerated rather than discarded as waste.

Representing new and long-standing companies, these examples cut across many industries.

See Appendix A for definitions of selected terminology (e.g., circular economy) used through this book.

Table 1: Industries in Transformation

Industry	Yesterday's (Linear) Focus	Tomorrow's (Circular) Focus
Aerospace	More flights; more fuel/carbon	More connection; less carbon
Apparel	Sell clothing	Sell; lease; take back clothing
Automotive	Sell cars and trucks	Sell mobility solutions
Chemicals	Make chemicals from hydrocarbons	Sell solutions; grow biomaterials & recycled products
Energy	More energy; more carbon	More energy; more efficiency; less carbon
Food & Beverage	More food that tastes good	More healthy food; less water; less waste
Hotels & Leisure	Sell lodging from a facility	Sell lodging solutions – including from a host
Industrial	Make; sell; and forget	Make; lease; take back; remanufacture
Information Technology	Sell equipment and services	Solve the world's toughest challenges
Mining	Mine ore	Mine landfills and warehouses (take back); recycle
Pharmaceuticals	Sell drugs	Sell health solutions
Retailing	Sell "stuff"	Sell solutions
Waste Services	Haul & dispose of waste in landfills	Sell, recycle, reuse; eliminate waste

Source: ✿ HEDSTROM
       ASSOCIATES

Given this backdrop, what are CEOs, Boards of Directors, and the executives advising them to do? Clearly, businesses across industry sectors need to be much more attentive to their surroundings and increasingly agile so as to adapt to volatile markets. Where to begin? *Change the sustainability conversation.*

A New Conversation about Sustainability

The sustainability conversation, as depicted on the left side of Figure 2, has been long dominated by environmental and social headlines. The vast majority of articles and books written about sustainability over the past 30 years have focused largely on the environment: degradation, resource limits, externalities, climate change, pesticides, toxics, and waste. How depressing!

Dozens of books describe the global environmental challenges, while too many business-oriented books paint a picture that sustainability is all about "win-win" and "green is gold." This is far too simplistic and often just not true. Moreover, not only has the subject been beaten to death, *it is the wrong conversation.*

Figure 2: The Changing Sustainability Conversation

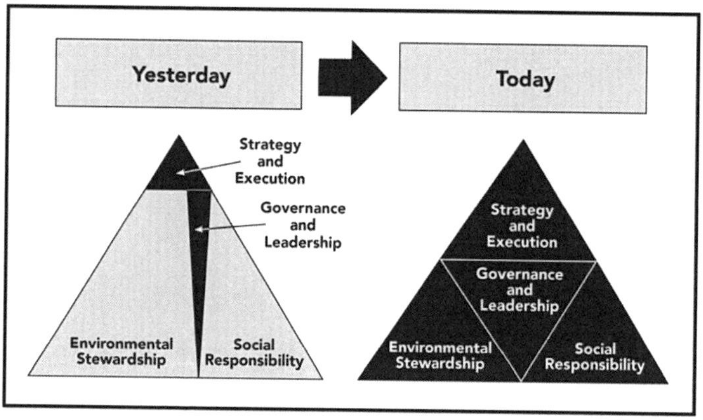

Source: HEDSTROM

The "right" conversation about sustainability focuses on corporate positioning and strategy. It begins with a deep examination of the megatrends impacting every company. As reported by the World Economic Forum in its annual

(2017) update,[10] *a number of the highest-risk megatrends are not only sustainability related but also focused squarely on climate change.* Four of the top five risks are: extreme weather events, failure of climate change mitigation and adaptation, water crises, and large-scale involuntary migration. These risks – interwoven with other societal challenges (e.g., inequality, technology impact of digital transformation on job creation, etc.) – will impact different industry sectors in different ways.

With the robust understanding of the ESG trends in hand, Board members, CEOs, and other top executives should examine questions like these: *As the sustainability transformation unfolds, how are we positioning ourselves? Are we at risk of "missing the boat" by doing business as usual? Will we, as with Borders Books overcome by Amazon.com, find ourselves saying, "Whoops. We missed that!"?* Former GE CEO Jeff Immelt recognized in 2004 that climate change would impact virtually every GE customer. Immelt saw a massive business opportunity, which GE subsequently launched (2005) as *Ecomagination.*

The Four-Stage Transformation Model
Engaging. Accelerating. Leading. Transforming.

Because sustainability is fundamentally about industry transformation, board members and C-suite executives have found it helpful to assess their company's current corporate sustainability position in terms of four stages – depicted in Figure 3. The four-stage transformation model described below refers to Hedstrom Associates' Corporate Sustainability Scorecard.

Note that the rating scale in the Corporate Sustainability Scorecard is a tough one. This is not your traditional rating scale where Stage 4 is the top quartile of companies today. The bell curve on this Scorecard is skewed left, reflecting the fact that the vast majority of companies today are early in their sustainability transformation. (See Figure 3.)

The four-stage transformation model helps companies assess and manage progress proactively through the "messy transformation." During the early stages, this involves engaging deeply with (and learning about) sustainability. Toward Stage 3 and Stage 4, it involves disruptive innovation – in the way that *Airbnb, Tesla,* and *Novelis* are transforming their industries.

Figure 3: Distribution of Global 500 Companies

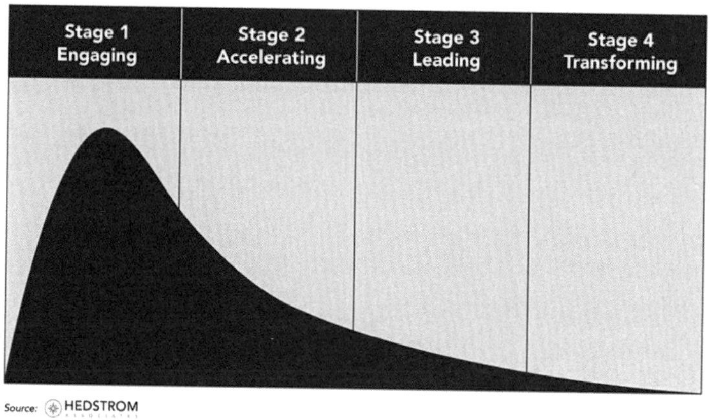

Stage 1 Engaging	Stage 2 Accelerating	Stage 3 Leading	Stage 4 Transforming

Source: ⊕HEDSTROM

An example of a summary scorecard for a typical company is depicted in Figure 4. See Appendix B for a description of each of 17 elements of the Scorecard depicted in Figure 4 (e.g., "CEO Leadership"). *A key point to keep in mind:* While it is convenient to express a company as being "in Stage 1" or "a Stage 2 company," in reality, most companies exhibit a range of attributes that fall across several stages of maturity on this scorecard.

Figure 4: Example Corporate Sustainability Scorecard

	Stage 1 Engaging	Stage 2 Accelerating	Stage 3 Leading	Stage 4 Transforming
Governance and Leadership	1	2	3	4
Vision, Mission, Values	← ● →			
CEO Leadership	← ● →			
Board of Directors Leadership	← ● →			
Goals and Metrics	← ● →			
Culture and Organization	← ●			
Stakeholder Engagement	← ● →			
Disclosure, Reporting, Transparency	← ● →			
Strategy and Execution	1	2	3	4
Strategic Planning	← ● →			
Innovation, Research and Development	← ● →			
Customers and Markets	← ● →			
Products, Services, and Solutions	← ● →			
Environmental Stewardship	1	2	3	4
Environmental Footprint – Operations	← ● →			
Supply Chain – Environmental Impacts	← ● →			
Environmental Footprint – Products	← ● →			
Social Responsibility	1	2	3	4
Own Operations: Workplace	← ● →			
Supply Chain Social Impacts	← ● →			
Community Investment	← ● →			

Source: ⊕ HEDSTROM

A brief synopsis of the characteristics of the four stages of transformation follows.

Stage 1 – "Engaging"

Stage 1 companies engage with sustainability issues in a variety of ways, although they do not change their company or their businesses fundamentally. These companies undertake important efforts to reduce impacts and drive EHS and social responsibility excellence. Sustainability efforts are often driven by the chief environment, health, and safety (EHS) officer in collaboration with the officer leading philanthropy and corporate citizenship initiatives. Environmental stewardship and social responsibility are considered the "right thing to do." Environmental management is largely about risk management. Social responsibility is about worker safety and health, diversity, community responsibility, and philanthropy.

Stage 1 companies are committed to compliance – not just with laws, regulations, and internal company standards, but also increasingly with industry codes of practice and de facto requirements, including the Global Reporting Initiative (GRI) sustainability reporting guidelines and other non-governmental organization (NGO) expectations. Stage 1 companies implement strong programs to reduce energy use, greenhouse gas (GHG) emissions, and waste in their own operations. They also respond to environmental and social pressures throughout their supply chain.

Stage 1 companies tend to interact primarily with their industry peers; and they typically support positions endorsed by their major industry associations. These companies may partner with external stakeholders on selected initiatives. Many, but not all, Stage 1 companies publish external EHS and/or sustainability reports (or the equivalent on their websites).

In summary, Stage 1 companies do many good things. However, when viewed in hindsight from those who are leaders, Stage 1 companies essentially *"dabble in sustainability,"* while they continue to make the same products they traditionally produced.

Stage 2 – "Accelerating"

As a key characteristic of Stage 2 companies, *the CEO explicitly recognizes the potential significance of sustainability – and launches a few key initiatives to position the company as a leader on a business-critical aspect of sustainability.* In some cases, the CEO sees sustainability issues not only as a source of risk, but also as a source of potential opportunity.

What separates Stage 2 companies from their Stage 1 counterparts? Notably, the CEO of a Stage 2 company personally stakes out a position that addresses a "material" environmental or social issue faced by the company and its industry. A *material* issue (Appendix A) is much more than an *important* issue. Many Stage 1 and Stage 2 companies publish a "materiality assessment" that may identify 20 to 40 or more *important* issues. Yet, in virtually every case, a company has only a small handful of *truly material* ESG issues. (See *Part Three: Environmental Stewardship* for a further discussion of materiality.)

In Stage 2 companies, the CEO may revise the company's vision, mission, and values (as *Ashland* recently did) to align more directly with the realities of 21st century growth. [Ashland's *old vision* was *"To be viewed as the best specialty chemical company in the world."* The company's *new vision* is *"To make a better world by providing creative solutions through the application of specialty ingredients and materials."*[11]] In some cases, Stage 2 companies set forth CEO-driven and bold sustainability positioning and goals. Many companies (e.g., *Alcoa, AT&T, Campbell Soup, FedEx, Ingersoll Rand,* and *J&J,* among others) have done this with their greenhouse gas reduction goals. The CEO and other senior executives may weave sustainability into public statements and speeches. In other situations, the company achieves a breakthrough position on a key issue facing its industry. For example, many Stage 2 companies took a lead role in addressing key industry challenges such as electronic waste and conflict minerals. As Stage 2 companies advance, they build a culture that values sustainability-related innovation. For example, they may focus on stakeholder partnerships on a major social or ecosystem issue.

Stage 2 companies have well-defined environmental and social management systems, though those processes tend to be *"bolted onto"* (rather than *"woven into"*) core business processes and business decisions. These companies have not changed their business models fundamentally. *Those in the manufacturing or process industries still largely operate in the traditional, linear, "take-make-waste" model*, as contrasted with the new circular economy model. Those in the lighter footprint and service sectors remain focused on traditional customers, rather than also focusing on emerging middle class customers (at the bottom of the economic pyramid).

Stage 3 – "Leading"

Stage 3 companies begin to transform their business portfolios to leverage sustainability opportunities. Moving beyond the few key CEO-driven sustainability initiatives of Stage 2 companies, the Stage 3 companies embody economist Joseph Schumpeter's concept of "creative destruction." They make strategic choices to divest "old economy" businesses and to invest in cleaner, greener, and more society-friendly enterprises.

Stage 3 companies take a longer-term view. They see the clean technology sector growing at double-digit rates – including products and processes that improve environmental performance in the construction, transport, energy, water, and waste industries. These companies want to be part of the "clean technology" revolution. They see massive growth opportunities in stabilizing atmospheric carbon concentrations, access to fresh water, clean transport, and smart cities. For example, more than any other major oil company globally, the French oil company, *Total*, sees electricity as a hedge against oil's eventual decline. Total is building a new business (akin to *Ford's* sustainable mobility business) around green energy, including batteries, solar, and other renewables.

Companies moving significantly into Stage 3 consider sustainability key to their organizations' long-term viability and value-creation. For example, *NextEra Energy* has made such a choice with its investments in renewable energy. Sustainability represents one or more platforms for top-line growth. A turning point for companies to focus in a major way on *product impacts* was in 2005 when *GE* launched *Ecomagination* – initially a line of GE products that offered customers superior environmental performance (especially lower use of energy) than competitor products. *Siemens* sees the transition to a low-carbon economy as the biggest industrial challenge of this century. The company's *Environmental Portfolio* grew to almost half (46 percent) of the company's annual revenue in 2016. Stage 3 companies have a clear, focused strategy that places global environmental and social drivers at the core. They anticipate customer needs and future differentiators, as *Toyota* did with the Prius many years ago. A Stage 3 company is viewed internally and externally as open, transparent, innovative, and critically aware of risks and opportunities (e.g., *SC Johnson* and *Nike* have been systematically removing toxic materials from their products).

In making the decision to implement such significant changes, CEOs of Stage 3 companies begin the hard work of **weaving material ESG issues into the fabric of every critical business process, key business decision, and investment.** The key here is *material* as opposed to *important* ESG issues. For example, it is not likely material for a bank to reduce its water consumption, while it is material to change its investment criteria or lending policy to better reflect the ESG risks of its customers. This turns out to be a massive effort, as anyone close to the transformation of *Novelis* or *Unilever* can attest.

Stage 4 – "Transforming"

Stage 4 companies are evolving rapidly as models of twenty-first century corporations. Those in the manufacturing or process industries (historically reliant on physical resources) live in the circular economy. For a pharmaceutical company, the issue is less about the circular economy and more about how many lives are improved as a result of access to medicines. Sustainability is incorporated fully into the Stage 4 company's vision, mission, culture, business model, and goals. Each of these companies has a clearly defined roadmap for sustainable growth and profitability, which explicitly reflects the firm's responsibility to future generations. This commitment extends far beyond the CEO. In Stage 4 companies, *sustainability is integrated fully within all aspects of the business* as they move toward 100 percent renewable energy, closed-loop manufacturing, shifting from product to service to solution, and enhancing employee and community health. The focus of these companies remains steadfast on long-term profitability and growth, while also helping to solving the world's toughest problems. *Tesla* CEO Elon Musk epitomizes this description. He points to Tesla's huge "gigafactory" in Nevada as a model for one way to *transition the entire world to sustainable energy.*

Though no major company today is solidly in Stage 4, a growing number of companies have some Stage 4 attributes. They fall into two groups: young, innovative, sharing-economy companies, such as *Airbnb, Google,* and *Tesla*; and old-line companies, such as *BASF, Philips, Siemens, Unilever,* and *Waste Management.*

Unilever (#150 on the 2017 Fortune 500 list) is well into its multi-year Sustainable Living Plan, which was launched in 2010 to "decouple" revenue growth and value creation from environmental and social impacts. This decoupling is driven by the company's 2030 goal: to cut in half the environmental impacts/footprint associated with making and using its products – as the company continues to grow its business. In 2012, Unilever CEO Paul Polman further drove the focus on long-term value creation when he stated at the World Economic Forum in Davos, "We don't do three-month (financial) reporting anymore."[12] Unilever has inspired many "smart follower" companies to grow their revenue while cutting their impacts and footprint.

Shortly after being named CEO of *Waste Management, Inc.*, in 2004, David Steiner and his management team faced what could be considered a nightmare. Increasingly, their customers were embracing the concept of "zero waste." That was good news for the environment, but not for the biggest trash hauler in the United States.

Consequently, Steiner looked for ways to extract value from the waste stream. The company introduced a new service: counseling large customers on how to reduce their waste. By 2017, "green services" accounted for half of Waste Management's revenue.

The Transformation Challenge

Transforming a company to be positioned for value creation in the sustainability era is incredibly challenging. It can be messy. While some CEOs appear to be successful in navigating this transformation, other CEOs have lost their jobs, arguably by moving too quickly. David Crane, the charismatic former CEO of power company NRG, is widely regarded as a sustainability visionary. He led NRG through a major transformation before finding that he and his Board could not agree on executing some of the key fundamentals of the business.

The transformation challenge is complicated by the impact of hedge funds. In early 2017, Unilever fended off a hostile bid by Kraft Heinz. However, Unilever's ability to survive challenges from private equity firms such as those that control Kraft Heinz is a story that is still playing out.

The Corporate Sustainability Scorecard™ C-Suite Rating System

The Corporate Sustainability Scorecard™ C-suite rating system was developed to facilitate discussions in the boardroom. The Scorecard is designed to help companies answer the same question many CEOs and board members have asked the author: *How do we stack up today vis-à-vis sustainability as compared with competitors, best practices, and where leading companies are heading*? The

Scorecard also helps executives map out *where they want their companies to be tomorrow* – given the competitive landscape, each company's ambitions, and the speed needed to win in the marketplace. The Scorecard is characterized as follows:

- *Robust.* The Corporate Sustainability Scorecard is simple in its summary form (Figure 4), though it is constructed as a comprehensive rating system supported by hundreds of "best practice" company examples. The Scorecard is organized into four parts: *Governance and Leadership, Strategy and Execution, Environmental Stewardship,* and *Social Responsibility.* Within those four parts, 17 topics (elements) comprise the overall Scorecard. Each element (e.g., "CEO Leadership") is defined in Appendix B. For each of the 17 elements of the Scorecard, executives rate the company on 8 to 12 sub-elements: Key Sustainability Indicators.

- *C-Suite Language.* The 17 individual elements that comprise the Corporate Sustainability Scorecard are purely business-focused. Each element (e.g., Culture and Organization; Strategic Planning; Innovation, Research and Development, etc.) is a major corporate function or activity on which CEOs and Boards of Directors spend considerable time. In other words, sustainability is *woven into* how businesses run – rather than *bolted on.*

- *Tried and Tested.* The Corporate Sustainability Scorecard builds on Gib Hedstrom's 30 years of experience working in the trenches with executives at over 250 companies in the United States, Europe, and

Asia. From 2000 to 2015, Hedstrom and his colleagues used variations of the Scorecard with executive sustainability teams at dozens of companies across a range of industries. In 2015, Hedstrom Associates ran a pilot initiative with several dozen Global 500 companies. Each company completed one or more self-assessments, participated in one to three webinars, and provided extensive feedback.

- *Balanced.* The Scorecard reflects the right-hand side of Figure 2. This means the Scorecard is *strong on governance and on strategy* – in stark contrast to the over 100 sustainability rating schemes in existence today. These schemes were developed by external stakeholders to encourage companies to disclose data on aspects of sustainability performance. In comparison, the Scorecard is focused on the aspects of running a business that matter most to Boards of Directors and C-suite executives.

- *Tough Rating Scale.* Fundamentally, sustainability is about the transformation of industries and companies. To help boards and C-suite executives navigate such change, the Scorecard has a tough rating scale. Based on the author's experience working with hundreds of companies globally over the past 30 years, Hedstrom Associates estimates that nearly half of all companies in the developed world are in Stage 1, while most of the remaining companies are in Stage 2.

- *Full of Best-Practice Company Examples.* Several hundred examples are provided of companies that are considered to be in Stage 3 or Stage 4 for a particular attribute.

See Appendix C for more detailed information about the Corporate Sustainability Scorecard.

The Scorecard has been used with the following companies in recent years: 3M, Air Products, Akzo Nobel, Anheuser-Busch, Ashland, Campbell Soup, Coca-Cola, Cytec, Deere, Dell, DuPont, Ford, Honeywell, HP, International Paper, Johnson & Johnson, Lockheed Martin, NextEra Energy, Novartis, Novelis, Novo Nordisk, Pemex, Raytheon, SC Johnson, Shell, Sims Metal Management, UPS, USG, and Xerox. (Note: in some cases, the Scorecard was used as part of a Hedstrom Associates client assignment for the company; in other cases, the company used the Scorecard on its own.)

Organization of the Book

Sustainability: A Guide for Boards and C-Suites is a succinct business-focused summary of how to think about the risks and opportunities associated with sustainability for your company. The book includes the author's insights not only from the approximately 60 board meetings he has participated in, but also from the experiences of over 50 companies that have used the Scorecard over the past 20 years.

A longer version of this book, the *Handbook for The Corporate Sustainability Scorecard*, is a companion guide for registered users of the Corporate Sustainability Scorecard [TM] C-suite rating system. The *Handbook* includes detailed rating templates for each element of the Scorecard depicted in Figure 4 and is used to create a company self-assessment on the website. It also includes the over 200 corporate "best practice" case examples found on www.TheSustainabilityScorecard.com.

The next four chapters of this book address the four main parts of the Scorecard: *Governance and Leadership*; *Strategy and Execution*; *Environmental Stewardship*; and *Social Responsibility*. Each chapter begins with an overview of the content; contains a description of today's current status; summarizes the opportunity for companies to excel; and ends with a brief summary of how "tomorrow's leaders...today" are implementing each element of the scorecard.

At the end of each chapter, a table lists the "Key Sustainability Indicators" that are used to evaluate a company on each element of the Scorecard. (See Figure 4, Appendix C, and www.TheSustainabilityScorecard.com.)

As you consider where your company (as well as your competitors and customers) sits across the four-stage model, keep these points in mind:

- *There is no inherently right or wrong place to be on this continuum.* The Corporate Sustainability Scorecard focuses on progressing through various stages. "Right" or "wrong" depends on timing. Certainly, examples exist of Stage 3 and Stage 4 companies that have faltered, and of Stage 1 and Stage 2 companies that have looked wise in hindsight.

- *The Scorecard rating scale is deliberately tough.* As depicted in Figure 4, the vast majority of companies today are in Stage 1 and Stage 2. The fundamental premise behind this Scorecard is that sustainability is about transformation; that is, virtually every old-school company must transform itself to survive and thrive.

- ***Don't be surprised if your company is largely in Stage 1.*** The majority of companies find that many attributes of their company are in Stage 1 today – or were until fairly recently. Even if your company is predominantly in Stage 2 or above, the chances are that you have many internal activities and core business processes that remain in Stage 1.

- ***Moving at the right speed at the right time is essential.*** Companies move at different speeds. *DuPont* began early and moved systematically from Stage 1 to Stage 3. *GE* decided in 2005 that it was "behind the game" and needed to leapfrog beyond competitors and peers as it moved very quickly from Stage 1 to Stage 3.

Part One:
Getting Sustainability Governance Right

Author's Sustainability Stories from the C-Suite and Boardroom...

Consider the story of one company that is "getting sustainability governance right."

At the request of the CEO of a major North American utility, I recently led a one-hour discussion titled "Sustainability and the Future" with the full Board of Directors. The conversation continued over dinner that evening. The next morning, I participated in a three-hour scenario planning exercise with the full board and executive team.

The purpose of the exercise was to determine how the company would respond to future disruption in its industry while meeting increasing stakeholder demands. The board members and leadership team "rolled up their sleeves" and dove into carefully developed scenario exercises. The executives explored how the company would fare in potential future worlds involving the two extremes of: (1) global attention to climate change and carbon reductions, and (2) technology developments (e.g., with renewables and storage technology). Groups of directors and executives (4-6 per group) explored how to succeed in four very different futures.

Quite honestly, I was astonished at how energetically and deeply the board members engaged! For several hours we had small group exercises, report-outs, and open discussion – quite the opposite of the "normal" highly orchestrated board meeting.

At the end of the morning, the board met in executive session as the rest of us left the room. When we returned, the Board Chair said that the sustainability conversations had been the best use of time he could remember at any board meeting. (That was quite a statement!) The Board had decided to add an extra half-day to their next full board meeting. The Chair summarized some instructions for the next steps.

Postscript: In the months since that meeting, the board increasingly has taken leadership of the sustainability agenda. The CSO was moved to the strategic planning team; and the CEO changed the corporate planning approach from the traditional "one-shot" annual event into a series of 12 monthly sessions over the year.

The core message to take away from this story is this: **it is possible for a sustainability director to change the boardroom conversation – and to do so dramatically.** The story above is notably different from traditional boardroom sustainability discussions, where many boards may spend only 30-60 minutes per year on the subject. In a recent Conference Board poll, 69 percent of companies responded that their board committee (or full board) typically spends two to four hours per year on sustainability/EHS issues.[13]

The Situation: Governance and Sustainability

Without "getting governance right," a company finds it difficult to get anything else right. This is true with creating successful products and services, creating robust brands, delivering consistent and strong financial results, and earning a reputation as "a good company to work for." *Increasingly, companies understand that this is true with sustainability too.*

So how do board members rate their effectiveness at sustainability? Until recently, by their own admission, board members did not score themselves well. In the 2009 National Association of Corporate Directors (NACD) survey of over 600 corporate board members, directors rated their effectiveness at sustainability (corporate social responsibility) almost "dead last" [20/21].[14] This has improved a bit since then. In its 2016-2017 Public Company Governance Survey, NACD found that of 631 public company responses, 33 percent say the board has spent too little time on sustainability over the past 12 months. Three in ten board members (29 percent) claim that a key barrier to a board's ability to oversee strategy is insufficient board of directors' understanding of the industry/environmental context affecting strategy. Yet, only 8 percent receive risk information from their sustainability function; and 11 percent of companies analyze sustainability-related measures for the purposes of senior executive compensation.[15]

Governance for a corporation essentially defines "how we run the place." It consists of the leadership structures, policies, processes, and practices affecting the way the CEO, Board, and senior management team run a corporation. It includes the goals, the culture and organization, and the relationships among the various stakeholders, including: shareholders, employees, suppliers, customers, banks and other lenders, regulators, the environment, and the community at large.

The third landmark report on corporate governance (King III) by the Institute of Directors in South Africa (the King Committee on governance) – the bellwethers of corporate governance – states...

"Sustainability is the primary moral and economic imperative of the 21st century. It is one of the most important sources of both opportunities and risks for businesses. Nature, society, and business are interconnected in complex ways that should be understood by business decision-makers. Most importantly, current incremental changes towards sustainability are not sufficient – we need a fundamental shift in the way companies and directors act and organize themselves".[16]

King III goes further than previous guidance. The report urges that the disclosure of sustainability performance be done through integrated financial and sustainability (environment, social, and governance) reports, which are overseen and evaluated by the audit committee of the board.

The Opportunity: Don't Fail the 80/20 Rule

Historically, "governance" has been largely absent from conversations about sustainability (Figure 5). Over time, the sustainability conversation evolved in two waves discussed below. The opportunity for companies today is to build robust governance processes that drive the full integration of sustainability / ESG into the core of the company.

First Wave – Triple Bottom Line: During the late 1990s and early 2000s, sustainability was characterized as the "triple bottom line" of environmental stewardship, social responsibility, and economic performance – sometimes referred to as "People, Planet, Profits." Here's the rub: *the* *"triple bottom line" does not mention governance.* Furthermore, the "profit" leg of sustainability has been given short shrift and rarely has been discussed in a comprehensive way.

Figure 5: Where is the "G" in the Triple Bottom Line?

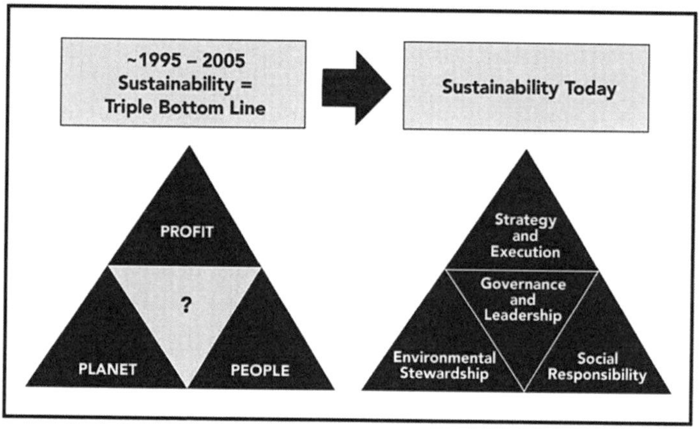

Source: HEDSTROM

Second Wave – Environmental, Social, and Governance (ESG): Around 2005, the mainstream investment community began to focus on carbon risk in particular, while starting to use the term "ESG" (referring to the environmental, social, and governance factors impacting an investment in a company) to characterize these risks. However, in looking a bit deeper, Hedstrom Associates finds that investors focus almost entirely on *governance data,* such as gender diversity of the board and executive ranks, or CEO compensation as a multiple of average employee compensation.

In the opinion of Hedstrom Associates, ESG, as practiced today, does a very poor job of focusing on **governance processes**. Anyone who has participated actively in C-suite and board of directors meetings knows that the vast majority of what constitutes "robust governance" is driven by robust governance processes. GE's Session C has been one excellent example: through its intense multi-level performance appraisal process, the CEO personally reviews GE's top several hundred officers every year.

Many companies examine the "governance" part of ESG with their annual Dow Jones Sustainability Index (DJSI) application. DJSI is constructed as a tool to help with investment decisions. However, by design, DJSI is not particularly focused on long-term strategy. Hedstrom Associates recently helped a client with every aspect of its DJSI submittal. We found that while DJSI makes some attempt to address corporate governance and business issues, DJSI heavily reflects the left side of Figure 2 (shown earlier). *The DJSI application focuses primarily on past data and correlations; DJSI has relatively little focus on the connection between sustainability and corporate strategy.* The governance section of DJSI focuses almost entirely on areas where there is **data** about governance. Focusing on governance data alone *fails the 80/20 rule*. In the Corporate Sustainability Scorecard, about 80 percent of the governance attributes are reflected in robust business *processes* – not in *data*.

Governance and Leadership at a Glance: Tomorrow's Leaders Today

Ironically, "getting governance right" is not difficult, nor does it require navigating uncharted waters. In a word, it is about *leadership*. Companies that are Stage 3 today in sustainability governance have made initial, significant steps toward transformation.

Below is a brief snapshot of how a few leading companies are addressing the seven key elements of sustainability and corporate governance –

- **Vision, Mission, Values:** Companies wanting to move beyond Stage 2 often start with *rethinking their vision, mission, and values*. *Intel* amended its corporate charter in 2010 to include sustainability. *Total*, the French oil giant, sensing peak demand for crude oil, declared in 2017 that "electricity is the energy of the 21st century." Total is transforming its portfolio and building tomorrow's cleaner, less carbon-intensive businesses alongside its traditional business.

- **CEO Leadership:** Tomorrow's leaders have *very strong, often bold leadership from the CEO*. Current or past CEOs of *DuPont, GE, IBM, Kingfisher, Marks & Spencer, Nike, Novelis, NRG, Unilever,* and *Walmart,* for example, have singlehandedly staked out a transformative position on sustainability. In some cases, the CEO moved too fast toward fully embracing sustainability. Phil Martens, former CEO of *Novelis,* embraced an "ethos of disruption" requiring a whole new way of thinking and operating. *NRG's* former CEO David Crane wanted to "transform our company, our industry, and society." In other companies' situations, the CEO may not be moving fast enough to integrate ESG into the core of the company. *Ford's* former CEO Mark Fields was pushed out in 2017; the new CEO James Hackett had been leading Ford's sustainable mobility businesses.

- **Board Leadership:** The boards of directors of Stage 3 companies *engage deeply with sustainability – and then they respond*. *Sims Metal Management,* the world's largest metal recycling firm, is positioned as a model circular economy company. The Board and CEO decided to demonstrate further commitment at the top by having the Board of Directors personally sign a commitment to sustainability.

  Having a strong sustainability voice on the external Board of Directors is one of the best ways to learn about sustainability. Notable examples have included: *Ashland* (Patrick Noonan, followed by John Turner), *International Paper* (Patrick Noonan), *DuPont* (Bill Riley), and *Nike* (Jill Ker Conway).

  Absent a sustainability expert on the Board, external sustainability advisors play a big role in informing the CEO, Board, and leadership team, while also serving as a sounding board for many aspects of strong governance, such as long-term goals, stakeholder relations, and reporting. *Dow Chemical* established an external sustainability advisory board in 1992 and a growing number of companies have followed suit, including: *Kimberly Clark (*2007), *Unilever (2010)*, and *Novelis* (2012).

- **Goals and Metrics:** Stage 3 companies *set bold, long-term sustainability goals directly addressing their top one, two, or three material issues* (such as *Coca-Cola* and water). These bold goals often stand in stark contrast to their industry peers. Stage 2 companies typically have a dozen or more ESG goals based on their materiality assessment; however, the goals are not particularly bold. As Stage 3 examples, *BT, Coca-Cola, Kingfisher, IKEA, Interface, Sony*, and *Tesco* all have goals of net neutral or net positive impact (at least in some material issues like carbon or forests).

- **Culture and Organization:** Stage 3 companies *drive a culture of innovation and sustainability through employee benefits and incentives.* *3M*'s "15 percent time" was launched in 1948 giving all employees the opportunity to pursue creative ideas in the workplace. Increasingly, that time is devoted to tomorrow's sustainability solutions. *Google* provides a host of sustainability-related incentives. *Intel* calculates each employee's bonus, in part, on sustainability results. *Walmart* engages its 2.2 million employees through My Sustainability Plan.

- **Stakeholder Engagement:** Stage 3 companies typically *engage in deep partnerships with one or more leading non-governmental organizations (NGOs).* *Walmart* has worked closely with the Environmental Defense Fund, as did *SC Johnson, McDonald's*, and *Starbucks* in prior years. *JPMorgan Chase* has provided major funding to NatureVest, which is The Nature Conservancy's impact investing program supporting water markets, green infrastructure, climate adaptation, sustainable agriculture, and more.

- **Disclosure, Reporting, and Transparency**: Issuing a sustainability report is fine, but in the Corporate Sustainability Scorecard C-suite rating system, that puts a company in Stage 1. It is the content of the report that matters, as well as the extent to which the report's key audience appreciates it. As companies move from Stage 1 through Stage 2 to Stage 3 and beyond, the audience for the sustainability report changes. For Stage 3 companies, a *primary audience is Wall Street*. Investors want short, concise, purely business-focused reports that demonstrate how the company plans to capture value from sustainability trends in the coming years. Stage 3 companies are moving rapidly toward integrated reporting as they incorporate ESG (environmental, social, and governance) issues into traditional financial reporting.

Key Sustainability Indicators: Governance and Leadership

The Corporate Sustainability Scorecard allows a user to rate a company on about 150 criteria – which Hedstrom Associates calls "Key Sustainability Indicators." (*See Appendix C for additional information.*) Table 2 provides a listing of the rating criteria (Key Sustainability Indicators) associated with Part 1 of the Corporate Sustainability Scorecard: Governance and Leadership.

Table 2: Rating Criteria for Governance and Leadership

Vision, Mission, Values
Public Statements
• CEO's View Regarding ("re") Role of Company in Society
• Sustainability in Corporate Vision & Mission
• Sustainability in Core Values & Corporate Policies
• Support of International Sustainability Charters/Commitments*
Private Actions to Reinforce Sustainability in Vision, Mission, Values
• Managing Long-Term Viability of Core Business(es)
• Key Business Decisions (KBDs)* tied to Core Values
External Recognition
• Sustainability Ratings/Rankings
• Ethics & Trust Ratings

[* Asterisk indicates words or phrases defined in Appendix A.]

Table 2 continued: Rating Criteria for Governance and Leadership

CEO Leadership
CEO Engagement with Sustainability <ul><li>Speeches on Sustainability by CEO and C-Suite Executives</li><li>CEO Messages re Sustainability to Shareholders</li><li>CEO/C-Suite Meetings with Customers re Sustainability</li><li>CEO/C-Suite Messages to Employees re Sustainability</li><li>CEO Sources of Sustainability Learning</li></ul> *Managing Board Agendas* <ul><li>Board Committee Agendas re Sustainability</li><li>Full Board Agendas re Sustainability</li><li>Board Pre-Reading/Pre-Work re Sustainability</li></ul> *Structuring the Sustainability Organization* <ul><li>C-Suite Roles re Sustainability</li><li>Executive Sustainability Council*</li></ul>

Board of Directors Leadership
Board of Directors' Sustainability Structure and Resources <ul><li>Board's Responsibility for Oversight of Sustainability</li><li>Board's Sustainability Commitment</li><li>Board's Sustainability Expertise</li><li>Board's External Sustainability Advisors</li></ul> *Board of Directors' Assurance Processes* <ul><li>Board ESG* Review of Key Business Decisions (KBDs)</li><li>Reporting to Board of Most Material* ESG Issues</li><li>Assurance Letter*/Annual Risk Review signed by Business Leaders</li></ul> *Board of Directors' Commitment of Time to Sustainability* <ul><li>Time Spent on Sustainability in Board Committee Meetings</li><li>Time Spent on Sustainability in Full Board Meetings</li><li>Board of Directors' Sources of Sustainability Learning</li></ul>

[* Asterisk indicates words or phrases defined in Appendix A.]

Table 2 continued: Rating Criteria for Governance and Leadership

Goals and Metrics
Goal-Setting Process   • Materiality* Assessment of Sustainability Impacts/Risks   • Philosophy re Sustainability Goals   • Stakeholder Input to Sustainability Goals   *Time Horizon of Sustainability Goals*   • Long-term (5-20 year) Sustainability Goals   • Ultimate (e.g., 2050) Sustainability Goals   *Content and Impact of Sustainability Goals*   • Magnitude of Footprint/Impact Reduction   • Tracking Revenue from Sustainability Products/Services   • Accounting for Most Material Externalities (e.g., Cost of Carbon)
Culture and Organization
Management Accountability for and Attention to Sustainability   • Executive Committee Role re Sustainability   • Sustainability Factored into Executive Compensation   • Communication to Employees re Sustainability   *Key Culture Indicators Related to Sustainability*   • Alignment of Employee Benefits with Sustainability   • Internal Reward and Recognition re Sustainability   • Promotion of Sustainable Lifestyles   • "Unwritten Rules of the Game"* re Sustainability   *Sustainability Organization*   • Chief Sustainability Officer (CSO)* Role   • CSO (or equivalent) Reporting Level   • Inclusion of Sustainability in Performance Goals and Job Descriptions

[* Asterisk indicates words or phrases defined in Appendix A.]

Table 2 continued: Rating Criteria for Governance and Leadership

Stakeholder Engagement
Why Engage?   • Approach to Stakeholder* Engagement   • Reasons for Stakeholder Engagement   *Who from the Company Engages?*   • Company Leader re Stakeholder Engagement   • NGO* Partnerships re Sustainability   • Interaction with Investors on Sustainability   *What to Engage On?*   • Engaging on Most Material Issues Across Supply Chain   • Scale of Stakeholder Engagement re Sustainability   *How and When to Engage?*   • Link Between Stakeholder Engagement & Business Strategy   • Time Spent by CEO with NGO Stakeholders
Disclosure, Reporting, Transparency
Disclosure of Sustainability Risks, Posture, Programs and Plans   • Company Outreach re Materiality Assessment   • Disclosure of Material Sustainability Impacts   *Reporting of Sustainability Progress and Performance*   • Sustainability in Annual Report   • Sustainability Report*   • Data Assurance / Verification   *Transparency*   • Outreach Posture, Tools and Techniques   • Public Policy Alignment with Sustainability Commitments   • Corporate Marketing & Advertising Approach re Sustainability

[* Asterisk indicates words or phrases defined in Appendix A.]

Part Two: Strategy and Execution

Author's Sustainability Stories from the C-Suite and Boardroom...

The first time I met with Ashland Inc.'s Board of Directors Committee overseeing the company's corporate responsibility issues, the company looked very different than it looks now. In the late 1990s, Ashland owned the specialty chemical business that defines the company today. At the same time, the company also owned Arch Coal, Ashland Petroleum Company, Ashland Distribution Company, APAC (an asphalt paving company), and Valvoline. Ashland was a holding company – holding not only diverse businesses but also extensive environmental and social risks.

Over a period of years as an outside advisor, I met with the Board Committee eight or ten times. At each meeting, I participated in the full meeting (normally two hours). Then, at the end, I often met in executive session with the outside directors. The Committee Chair was long-time environmental leader Patrick F. Noonan, former President of The Nature Conservancy and Chairman of The Conservation Fund.

Without divulging confidential conversations, imagine the boardroom conversations in the late 1990s regarding Arch Coal and the long-standing practice in the coal industry of "mountain-top removal," essentially stripping off the top of mountains to access the coal seams below. Imagine too the conversations about Ashland's petroleum business, when BP (then) CEO John Browne had just spoken publicly about the need for oil companies to adopt a precautionary approach to climate change.

Working alongside the company's Vice President, Environment, Health and Safety, I gave the CEO and the executive team a primer on climate change in the late 1990s. We were not advocating any position, but rather summarizing the science and business risks and opportunities as best we knew at the time. Not surprisingly, the President of Arch Coal took strong exception to our remarks, quoting "experts" who denied climate science. At the end of that presentation, the Arch Coal President was the first one to ask for a copy of our slides.

Postscript: Fast forward 20 years and we see a story of transformation. Today the company's vision is "to make a better world by providing creative solutions through the application of specialty ingredients and materials."

[Note: the author's conversations with company executives – and especially his participation in board meetings – are strictly confidential. Every comment in this book about my interactions with a specific corporate board has been shared publicly by corporate executives of that company.]

The key message from this story is for companies to **"Lyft yourself before you get Kodak'd."** This requires C-suite and board conversations about how to transform the company to be leaner, more fit, and a less carbon-intensive 21st century winner.

The Situation: Beyond ESG

When the mainstream investment community finally began to latch on to sustainability in about 2005, it was through the lens of ESG (environment, social, and governance). Today, it is striking that ***ESG, as a descriptor of sustainability, remains inherently silent on corporate strategy and execution.*** Somehow, the "economic leg" of the *People - Planet - Profits* sustainability stool was simply replaced with governance. Moreover, as discussed in the last chapter, governance is by far the weakest link of the traditional ESG definition of sustainability. As Figure 6 illustrates, the ESG characterization of sustainability misses the vitally important dimension of weaving ESG issues into corporate strategy and execution.

Figure 6: Where is Strategy in ESG?

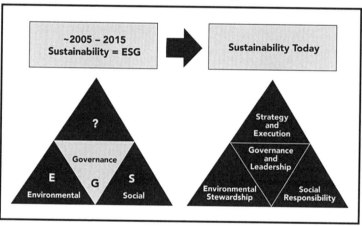

Source: HEDSTROM

As many CEOs and board members have underscored in their discussions with Hedstrom Associates, a company cannot be "sustainable" unless it generates sustained profits. Companies achieve that by executing a robust strategy. It does not matter whether environmental or social drivers are the main reason for key business decisions (e.g., portfolio changes; buying and selling companies). In the experience of Hedstrom Associates, if a Board pays careful attention to ESG issues alongside other business issues in a balanced and thoughtful way, the company is likely positioned well for future (sustainable) growth and profitability.

Embedding sustainability into strategy is the *single most significant place* where companies fall short vis-à-vis sustainability. Importantly, CEOs recognize this gap. In The Conference Board CEO Challenge 2016 survey, four of the top five strategies mentioned by CEOs globally for meeting the sustainability challenge relate directly to *embedding sustainability into corporate strategy*.[17]

The Opportunity: Strategy and Sustainability (Two Sides of the Coin)

Still today, there are two sides to the sustainability coin. Companies can drive ESG considerations into their core business and strategy by *reducing cost or risk* and by *growing sales and options for future growth*. Examples abound –

- *Reducing cost*: *3M, Dow Chemical*, and *DuPont* have cut waste and saved millions for decades. *Herman Miller* has committed to zero waste by 2023 with 50 percent of its power from renewables. *Dell* achieved a 95 percent "recycle and reuse" rate in 2014.

- *Reducing risk*: The potential risk presented by climate change caught the attention of *Swiss Re* and *Munich Re* over a decade ago. It caught *ExxonMobil's* attention in

May 2017 when 62 percent of Exxon shareholders voted against management and for the company to be more open about the impact of climate change on its business. ExxonMobil executives sought to head off the proposal, which was backed by 38 percent of shareholders in 2015 (and therefore failed). Smart companies have exited profitable businesses and product lines to reduce risk – as *3M* did in 2000 when the company decided to phase out production of chemicals PFOA and PFOS in Scotchgard.

- *Growing sales*: Over the past decade, a dozen or more very large multinational companies have demonstrated that they can grow revenue through a defined set of products, services, and solutions that are environmentally or socially preferred over the typical products in that family. (See Table 3 and access a recent Conference Board report for more information.[18])

- *Creating options for future growth*: *Avis* purchased *Zipcar* to position itself for growth in the sharing economy. *Cisco* and other companies view the "smart grid" as representing a $400 billion market by 2020. *Croda* (UK) considers sustainability a key differentiator and growth driver. *Terracycle* CEO Tom Szaky has built the company by working with large customers to recycle/upcycle their waste packaging into reusable products.

Table 3: Company Sustainable Product, Service, and Solution Portfolios

Examples of Company Sustainable Product, Service, and Solution Portfolios
Provided below are examples of how a range of industry leaders are transforming their product and service offerings toward tomorrow's circular economy focus.
• *BASF's* Accelerator Solutions accounted for 23 percent of BASF's relevant sales in 2014, or about €15 billion.
• *Caterpillar's* portfolio of sustainable products generated almost $10 billion in 2014 and accounted for 18 percent of the company's total revenue.
• *Dow's* portfolio of products that are highly advantaged by sustainable chemistry reached sales of $12.4 billion in 2015, accounting for 25 percent of total 2015 revenue.
• *DSM's* ECO+ solutions accounted for 57 percent of the company's total sales in 2015. ECO+ sales have an average annual growth rate of about 10 percent, and across several of DSM's businesses, ECO+ sales have higher margins than do non-ECO+ sales. Today, ECO+ and People+ are combined into the "Brighter Living Solutions" portfolio, which in 2016 accounted for 63 percent of total sales.
• *GE's* Ecomagination portfolio generated $36 billion in revenue in 2015, up from $18 billion in 2010. Ecomagination now accounts for one-third of GE's industrial segment revenue.
• *Johnson & Johnson's* Earthwards® portfolio grew from 9 products in 2009 to 85 products in June 2016. This portfolio represented over $9 billion in revenue and about 13 percent of the company's 2015 revenue.
• *Kimberly-Clark's* ecoLOGICAL portfolio accounted for 52 percent of the company's revenue in 2014 (up from 10 percent in 2010), or more than $10 billion.

Table 3 continued: Company Sustainable Product, Service, and Solution Portfolios

• *Kingfisher* (the UK-based home improvement company) derived 28 percent of sales from eco products in 2016 with a target of 50 percent by 2020.
• *Philips'* "green products" accounted for 64 percent of the company's overall revenue in 2016.
• *Siemens'* Environmental Portfolio accounted for almost €36 billion (46 percent of the company's overall revenue in 2016).
• *Toshiba's* sales of "Excellent Environmentally Conscious Products" rose from $3.6 billion in 2011 to $24 billion in 2015 (accounting for 42 percent of 2015 revenue).

The place to start always is to reduce cost and risk: the low-hanging fruit. Many companies have used these savings to fund investments in other areas of sustainability.

The exciting sustainability conversation is not about "doing less bad" by reducing impacts; instead, it is about *growth*. As the megaforces of middle class population growth, climate change, resource scarcity, and impact of externalities play out in the coming decades, companies can position themselves to grow and profit from these trends. Across a range of industries, *traditional* and *next-generation* companies have begun to unleash the power of innovation – driven by ESG issues – as a way to drive sustained profitability and growth.

Strategy and Execution at a Glance: Tomorrow's Leaders Today

When surveyed, most CEOs say they have a sustainability strategy. Yet dig a little deeper and that "strategy" likely includes sustainability reporting, some basic footprint reduction goals, a materiality assessment, and a host of programs and initiatives. In the experience of Hedstrom Associates, *the vast majority of companies lack a process that hard-wires the most material ESG (environmental, social, and governance) issues to its corporate strategy.*

Part One reviewed the critical components of a robust sustainability governance system, including the critical need for leadership at the top. *Part Two* of the Scorecard addresses strategy. Below is a brief snapshot of how a few leading companies are addressing the four key elements of how sustainability is factored into corporate strategy and execution –

- **Strategic Planning:** Stage 3 companies *do not have a separate sustainability strategy; they have embedded sustainability squarely into their core business strategy.* They use a robust scenario planning process (as *Shell* is famous for and companies like *Nike* and *PepsiCo* have emulated). Importantly, they factor ESG issues into *key business decisions,* defined as the handful of major decisions a company makes each year that typically require board of directors "sign-off." *3M* did this in 2000 when the company decided to phase out chemicals PFOA and PFOS in Scotchgard. *Swiss Re* and *Munich Re* did this with climate change more than a decade ago.

- **Innovation, Research, and Development:** Stage 3 companies *see innovation as core to their future. They see sustainability as the main driver of innovation.* *Tesla* was created to accelerate the advent of sustainable transport. *Akzo Nobel* is developing products that use CO_2 as a source material. *Dell* is using recycled ocean plastics in packaging. *Philips* is using drone technology for wind farm inspection. *Toyota* is using pollution-reducing billboards in California. *XL Hybrids* retrofits vans and trucks into hybrids, thereby reducing emissions and fuel use by 20 percent. *Walmart* convened over a dozen CEOs of major companies and CEOs of leading NGOs to sign new commitments accelerating innovation in sustainable agriculture and recycling.

- **Customers and Markets:** Stage 3 companies *work in new and different ways with customers.* GE launched Ecomagination purely in response to meeting customer needs (lower life-cycle energy costs) in the face of emerging mega-trends (environmental degradation and climate change). *Unilever* holds "Big Moments" events to make *sustainable living* commonplace. *Waste Management's* transformation from waste disposal to waste services was driven by a combination of attention to early signals of a customer trend and a CEO's major strategic thrust to respond to those needs (to move toward zero waste). *Allianz* (Brazil) home insurance provides a range of green services: energy and water efficiency; solar power; and recycling – including home collection service. *Natura Cosmeticos* (Brazil) launched Programa Amazonia, a 1.7-million-square-meter closed-cycle industrial complex in the Amazon region. *Novo Nordisk's* (Denmark) Changing Diabetes program in China educated 280,000 patients, trained 55,000 physicians, and grew its market share in insulin by 23 percent. *NTT Docomo* (Japan) aims to be a "Smart Life Partner" for its customers, deploying a wide range of health-related services (e.g., monitor their customers' exercise and diet).

- **Products, Services, and Solutions:** Stage 3 companies *decouple "product resource intensity" from sales*. They drive revenue growth through sustainable products and services – without growing the full life-cycle product footprint.[19] They shift from selling products to selling services and solutions. *Ashland's* new vision is to sell solutions (not chemicals). *Michelin* is moving to sell "distance" (a service), not only tires. Today's leaders are selling sustainable products, services, and solutions to existing markets (e.g., *Campbell Soup, Siemens, Philips, GE*), to new markets (e.g., *Cisco* with smart grid; *Schneider Electric* and *IBM* with smart cities), and into emerging markets. Many people think of *Apple* as primarily selling products. However, Apple reported in August 2017 that revenue from services (as opposed to products) accounted for more than $27.8 billion for the 12 months ending July 1, 2017 – making their "services" the equivalent of a Fortune 100 company.

Key Sustainability Indicators: Strategy and Execution

Table 4 provides a list of the rating criteria (Key Sustainability Indicators) associated with Part 2 of the Corporate Sustainability Scorecard: Strategy and Execution.

Table 4: Rating Criteria for Strategy and Execution

Strategic Planning
Sustainability Positioning and Strategy   • Corporate Sustainability Positioning   • Corporate Sustainability Strategy   *Business Drivers for Sustainability Within the Company*   • Sustainability Strategy re Cost Reduction   • Sustainability Strategy re Risk Reduction   • Sustainability Strategy re Revenue Generation   • Sustainability Strategy re Brand/Reputation Enhancement   *Sustainability Inputs to Corporate Planning Process(es)*   • Issues Analysis Process   • Use of Scenario Planning   • Sustainability Impact of Capital Expenditures
Innovation, Research, and Development
Role of Sustainability and Innovation   • Linkage Between Sustainability and Innovation   • Sustainable Innovation through Material and Labor Inputs   • Sustainable Innovation through Technology   *Processes and Methodologies*   • Sustainability Innovation Process   • Sustainable Innovation Tools   • Sustainability R&D Partnerships   *Sustainable Innovation Investments*   • R&D Investment in Sustainable Products   • Sustainability Investment Criteria

Table 4 continued: Rating Criteria for Strategy and Execution

Customers and Markets
Sustainability Linkage to Customers • Posture & Interaction with Customers re Sustainability • Identifying Customers' Sustainability Issues *Core Approach* • Customer Partnerships re Sustainability • Customer Communications and Satisfaction *Shaping Future Market Opportunities* • Selling Sustainability Features into Existing Markets • Selling Sustainability Features into Developing Markets
Products, Services, and Solutions
Basic Product Positioning • Product, Service, Solution (PSS)* Model • Societal Value of Products, Services, and Solutions • Product Responsibility Strategy • Sustainability in the Product Development Process • Product Sustainability Rating Process *Existing Products, Services, and Solutions* • Sustainability in Product Design • Product Quality and Safety • Product Sustainability Audits • Product Marketing and Advertising *Future Products, Services, and Solutions* • Sustainability Attributes in Product Line Extension • New Sustainable Product Families

[* Asterisk indicates words or phrases defined in Appendix A.]

Part Three: Environmental Stewardship

Author's Sustainability Stories from the C-Suite and Boardroom...

In 2001, I was almost "kicked out" of Oklahoma for mentioning climate change. In my final year at consulting firm, Arthur D. Little, I was leading a high-profile consulting assignment for the CEO of Kerr McGee. (Since that time, the oil and gas and chemical company sold its chemical operations by IPO as "Tronox" in 2005. The balance of the company was purchased by Anadarko Petroleum Corporation in 2006. The company no longer exists today.)

The CEO had five business transformation teams that each focused on a major corporate function. I was the senior advisor to the Environment team comprising six senior executives from across the company. Our team identified four areas that could have a significant cost or risk impact on the company. One of those areas was captured as "environmental strategy." Taking pride in its strong compliance posture, the company wanted to be a leader.

Interviewing the Senior Vice President of Strategy, I asked what he thought a leadership posture on climate change might look like. I set the context with the company's North Sea oil and gas competitor, BP, whose public posture on climate change was quite aggressive. BP's CEO at the time, John Browne, publicly stated his position that it was reasonable to take a precautionary approach to limiting greenhouse gas emissions.

Sitting in a corner office on the executive floor of the Kerr McGee Building in Oklahoma City, I realized that this SVP was the CEO's right-hand advisor. Along with the Presidents of the oil and chemical businesses and the CEO, they comprised the Executive Leadership Team. I asked the Senior Vice President a few strategic questions about carbon-related risk and opportunity. He looked me in the eye and said, "Don't ever mention climate change around here" (implying in this company or this city).

Postscript: Six weeks later, our team was able to have a business-focused conversation about climate change and environmental strategy. A Kerr McGee UK production manager from the North Sea operations was in Oklahoma and joined one of our presentations to the Executive Leadership Team. He was the one who brought up climate change. Furthermore, he completely surprised the CEO and C-suite executives when he stated that Kerr McGee UK actually had a position statement (similar to BP's) on climate change.

As this story shows, **sustainability involves tough – and evolving – conversations**. If a company is not having those conversations, those in charge probably are dancing around the edges of the core ESG issues.

The Situation: Overdose on Environmental Issues

Environmental stewardship depicted in Figure 7 (same as Figure 2 in the *Introduction*) has long dominated the sustainability headlines in the United States. The vast majority of articles and books written about sustainability over the past 30 years have focused largely on the environment: degradation, resource limits, externalities, climate change, pesticides, toxics, and waste. In Europe for comparison, environmental and social issues tend to be more balanced.

The starting point for every company's approach to environmental stewardship should be to conduct a robust materiality assessment. A materiality assessment (as noted in Part 1 – Governance) should be the basis for considering sustainability goals and metrics, as well as the associated programs, initiatives, and performance incentives that drive actions to meet those goals.

Figure 7: The Changing Sustainability Conversation

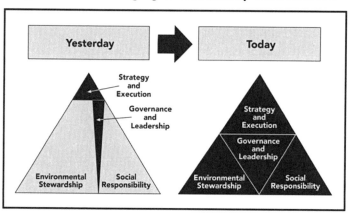

Source: HEDSTROM

However, this is where things go amiss for so many companies. The Global Reporting Initiative (GRI) uses the term "materiality" in a way that actually reinforces the lopsided sustainability conversation depicted on the left side of Figure 8. GRI defines materiality in a far broader way than investors have defined the term for decades.

- GRI defines materiality as a threshold for what they believe is **important** to be reported: *"The report should* *cover aspects that reflect the organization's significant environmental and social impacts; or that substantively influence the assessments and decisions"* of the various stakeholders.

• Investors define materiality as a key threshold for making investment decisions.

As a result of this GRI definition, the vast majority of sustainability reports today include a materiality matrix. (See Figure 8 for one example.) Many companies include as many as 30 or 50 environmental and social issues on their reported materiality matrix. Though these issues are *important*, the vast majority of them are not *material* (in the financial sense of the word).

Figure 8: Example Materiality Matrix

Low Impact, High Concern	Medium Impact, High Concern	[Material Issues] High Impact, High Concern
Low Impact, Medium Concern	Medium Impact, Medium Concern	High Impact, Medium Concern
Low Impact, Low Concern	Medium Impact, Low Concern	High Impact, Low Concern

Increasing Concern to Stakeholders →

Increasing Current or Potential Impact on Company →

Source: HEDSTROM

An excellent report on "Sustainable Development Key Performance Indicators (SD-KPIs),"[20] initially developed for the German Environment Ministry, identifies the top three material ESG indicators for each of 68 different industries.

This report aligns with Hedstrom Associates' view that the vast majority of companies have only one to four environmental or social issues that are truly *material* (in the financial sense of the word). For example, *Chevron, Duke Energy,* and *General Motors* are essentially "single issue" companies (and industries): that material issue is carbon/GHG. The material issues of *BASF* or *Dow Chemical* are typically safety, toxics, and carbon/GHG. For *Coca-Cola* or *Pepsi*, the material issues are water, obesity, carbon/GHG, and packaging waste.

The Sustainability Accounting Standards Board (SASB) is working to develop and disseminate sustainability accounting standards that help corporations disclose information to investors. SASB standards address the ESG (environmental, social, and governance) topics that are "reasonably likely" to have material impacts on the financial condition or operating performance of companies in an industry. SASB recognizes that each company is responsible for determining what information is "material" and what information should be included in filings with the U.S. Securities and Exchange Commission (SEC). In identifying sustainability topics that are reasonably likely to have material impacts, SASB applies the definition of "materiality" established under the U.S. securities laws.[21]

When companies define ESG materiality narrowly – as only a handful of truly material issues or impacts – they facilitate a conversation with the C-suite about strategy. Indeed, shortly after Jeff Seabright (current Chief Sustainability Officer at Unilever) arrived at *Coca-Cola* as VP Environment and Water and launched a major water initiative, the CEO added "water" as one of the company's major strategic thrusts.

The Opportunity: Simplify and Think Value Chain

Every company is responsible today, like it or not, for the full environmental footprint of its products, services, and solutions across the supply chain. The days are over for a company to own responsibility only for its wholly-owned or majority-owned operations. Instead, *Ford, GM,* and *Toyota* own the carbon impact of consumers as they drive their cars and trucks. *McDonald's* and *PepsiCo* own their contribution to the obesity epidemic. *Starbucks* is responsible for how much water and pesticides are used to grow its coffee beans – as well as the labor practices involved. *Tesco* and *Walmart* own the ecological impact of producing the food and beverages they sell.

The opportunity for chief sustainability officers and those communicating with the C-suite and board about sustainability is to frame and discuss environmental issues in the context of the supply chain.

- Manufacturing companies manage their business activities across the supply chain: defined as the movement and storage of raw materials, work-in-process inventory, and finished goods from point of origin to point of consumption.

- Companies in the service sector focus particularly on the value chain; those steps along the chain where value is created as distinct from steps where material is moved.

Regardless of industry, many companies are organized around key functions that include sourcing, production, distribution, sales, and customer service. It is very common in companies across industries today to have senior officers in charge of supply chain, procurement, operations, marketing, sales, etc.

Figure 9 illustrates key stages of a typical industry supply chain. (For purposes of simplicity, this figure assumes that "transportation" in or out of each step of the value chain is incorporated into those steps.)

Figure 9: Typical Industry Supply Chain

Source: HEDSTROM

While NGOs and many chief sustainability officers tend to think of sustainability by issue (carbon, water, waste, etc.), C-suite executives think of environmental stewardship the way they run the company, that is, across the supply chain. As a result, in the Corporate Sustainability Scorecard C-suite rating system, the many environmental issues across the supply chain are organized into three buckets: own operations footprint; supplier footprint; and product footprint.

For most companies, the large majority of the full life-cycle environmental impacts occur in only: (a) one or two areas of environmental impact, e.g., carbon/GHG; toxics, water, etc.; and (b) one key part of the supply chain, e.g., supplier, own operations, product use, and disposal. For example, *Ford, GM,* and *Toyota* have the vast majority of their impact in *product use* and *energy/carbon*. (Ford has stated that 85-90 percent of its carbon impact occurs in a customer's use of its products.)

Environmental Stewardship At a Glance: Tomorrow's Leaders Today

Today's Stage 3 companies excel in the environmental dimension of sustainability across three dimensions: their own operations, their suppliers, and their products.

We mentioned in the last chapter on strategy that sustainability is two sides of a coin: one side represents *risk*, and the other represents *opportunity*. Moreover, every company must focus first and foremost on risk: reducing the "bad stuff" not only in your own company's operations, but also throughout the supply chain. However, Stage 3 companies also see sustainability as a *source of innovation* to drive top-line revenue growth.

Part One reviewed the critical components of a robust sustainability governance system; and *Part Two* addressed how sustainability is factored into corporate strategy and execution. *Part Three* addresses environmental stewardship, organized around the supply chain. Below is a brief snapshot of how a few leading companies are addressing the three key elements of environmental stewardship –

- **Environmental Footprint – Operations:** Today's leaders are ***driving relentlessly toward "zero waste" in managing their own operations***. They are reducing or eliminating hazardous waste, achieving or working toward zero waste to landfills (*Caterpillar, P&G,* and *Subaru*), and working toward becoming carbon neutral (*Adobe Systems, Google, IKEA,* and small companies like *Curtis Packaging*). Companies as diverse as *General Mills* and *Novelis* are committed to sourcing their raw materials sustainably. *Kering* (France) and *Nike* have committed to phasing out all hazardous chemicals. *IKEA* and *Kingfisher* (UK) are following a roadmap to become "forest positive" (creating more forest than they use). *Johnson Controls* and *Telus* (Canada) manage their buildings for zero impact.

- **Supply Chain Environmental Impacts:** Stage 3 companies have taken bold steps to *green their supply chains.* *Walmart*, since 2005, relentlessly has driven "green" forward by demanding, for example, that suppliers reduce their packaging, hazardous materials, and water use. *P&G* and *Kaiser Permanente* followed *Walmart's* lead and made similar demands on suppliers. *Natura Cosmeticos* (Brazil), *Compass Group* (UK), *Hershey,* and *Rio Tinto* (UK) demanded that their suppliers protect biodiversity. *Baxter*, *HP,* and *Owens Corning* led their industries in setting supply chain sustainability goals. *Dell* is using certified closed-loop recycled plastics in its computers. *Adidas, Anvil Knitwear,* and *Nike* (among others) put in place processes to verify the performance of their suppliers.

- **Environmental Footprint – Products:** Stage 3 companies have, for years, *systematically reduced the environmental footprints of their products*. *SC Johnson* was an early leader: its Greenlist program evaluates material components of the company's products, and systematically phases out more hazardous ones. In the 1990s, *Electrolux* and *Ikea* offered a green product line. *Desso* (Netherlands) adopted a cradle-to-cradle approach in 2007. Today, many companies clearly are Stage 3 in at least one sustainable product attribute. Leaders in selected product attributes include: energy efficiency (*EMC* and *HP*), traceability (*Hershey* and *Patagonia*), material use (*Adidas* and *Herman Miller*), durability (*Autodesk* and *DuPont*), and recyclability (*Electrolux* and *Shaw Industries*). Finally, leaders in diverse industry sectors have staked out a leadership position in end-of-life product responsibility, such as *BMW* for vehicles and *Sprint* for cellphones.

Of course, one company's products are often another company's material inputs. *Walmart* imposes strict requirements on its suppliers, which becomes a supplier issue for Walmart and a product issue for *Dell, HP, Proctor & Gamble*, and other suppliers that are required, for example, to reduce or take back their packaging material.

Key Sustainability Indicators: Environmental Stewardship

Table 5 provides a listing of the rating criteria (Key Sustainability Indicators) associated with Part 3 of the Sustainability Scorecard: Environmental Stewardship.

Table 5: Rating Criteria for Environmental Stewardship

Environmental Footprint
Managing Purchased Resource Inputs • Chemical Substances Sourced • Energy Consumed (e.g., fuel, electricity, transport, etc.) • Materials Sourced: Biological-based (e.g., forest products, etc.) • Materials Sourced: Human-made (e.g., metals, plastics, etc.) • Water Sourced *Managing Own Physical Footprint* • Buildings and Equipment • Land Management (e.g., biodiversity, forest products, remediation and restoration) *Managing Non-Product Outputs* • Greenhouse Gas (GHG) Emissions (Scope 1) • Other Emissions • Waste Generation • Water Discharges
Supply Chain – Environmental Impacts
Posture and Management Processes • Posture re Supplier Environmental Footprint • Standards for Supplier Environmental Footprint • Measuring Supplier Environmental Footprint • Verifying Supplier Environmental Footprint *Addressing the Most Material Supply Chain Environmental Impacts* • Supplier Impacts: Biodiversity • Supplier (Indirect) GHG Emissions (Scope 2) • Supplier Impacts: Materials • Supplier Impacts: Toxics • Supplier Impacts: Water *Nature and Extent of Supplier Sustainability Partnerships* • Engaging with Suppliers • Setting Sustainability Goals with Suppliers

Table 5 continued: Rating Criteria for Environmental Stewardship

Environmental Footprint – Products
Overall Product Stewardship Approach • Product Stewardship Philosophy • Product Risk/Life-Cycle Assessments • Use of Industry Codes, Standards, Certifications, Eco-labels *Product Design Process* • Product Traceability • Product Energy Efficiency • Product Materials Use • Product Durability • Product Biodegradability • Product Recyclability / Reusability • Product Water-Use Efficiency *End-of-Life Product Management* • Packaging • End-of-Life Product Responsibility

Part Four: Social Responsibility

Author's Sustainability Stories from the C-Suite and Boardroom...

I had the opportunity to spend two weeks in Papua New Guinea in the late 1990s. This was a starkly different physical and social setting from anything I had yet experienced. As a member of a high-level executive audit team, we were charged with assessing the environmental status of the controversial Ok Tedi mining operation for BHP Billiton (then BHP).

The Ok Tedi mine was critically important to BHP. One of the largest copper mines in the world, the mine was (at the time of our visit) about 15 years through its useful life of 30 years. Moreover, the mine was facing considerable pressure for environmental reasons. Despite being located in one of the most remote places in the world, Ok Tedi was in the crosshairs of NGOs in Asia. The mine was located about 6,000 feet above sea level, in a rainforest area on geologically "new" soil, which was easily eroded (the opposite of granite).

The environmental issues at Ok Tedi were mind-boggling, so much so that BHP actually had a staff of about 30 full-time environmental scientists and experts at the site. They had commissioned major ecosystem studies examining the impacts of tailings runoff into the Fly River – one of the most fertile fishing grounds in the South China Sea.

For two weeks, we reviewed compliance records; took helicopter rides up and down the river systems; and met with local community groups. Then we came to a surprising conclusion: on paper, the Ok Tedi mine appeared to be largely or completely in compliance with PNG laws and regulations.

Yet, late one evening sitting around a conference room table, I stood up and went to a copy of the Corporate Environmental Policy hanging on the wall. I set it on the table so that all of us could read the words. The company's environmental policy, like that of most peer companies, included a general statement about "commitment to protecting the environment." We zeroed in on the actual words in the policy statement. After some heated discussions, our team developed a list of findings and recommendations.

<u>Postscript</u>: In the end, our report made it to the highest levels of the company. Not long after, BHP began divesting itself of the Ok Tedi mine and taking major financial charges against operations.

The message from this story: ***Social issues are complex, intertwined with environmental issues, and owned not only by the parent company but also throughout the value chain***. *Nike* owned the child labor issues in the late 1990s that led to a Supreme Court lawsuit; *Apple* owned the Foxconn labor and environmental abuses a decade ago; and every company that purchased copper sourced at Ok Tedi owned the social and environmental issues in Papua New Guinea.

The Situation: Looking Back – Not Looking Ahead

From its beginning, the socially responsible investing (SRI) movement has had social issues at its core – as the name implies. Early and long-standing leaders like Calvert focused as much or more on social issues as on environmental matters.

The "social dimension" of sustainability has grown in importance across many industry sectors as they take responsibility for ESG issues across their supply chains. The Nike, Inc. v. Kasky lawsuit that reached the U.S. Supreme Court in 2003 brought to the forefront how major corporations are responsible for far more than their own operations. Moreover, that lawsuit also raised visibility for human rights and related conditions. Supply chain issues pushed the social dimension of sustainability to a point of "roughly equal" weighting as the environmental issues – although this varies significantly by industry sector.

Globally, the environmental and social dimensions of sustainability tend to receive roughly equal focus. However, for many U.S. industry sectors, social responsibility (as depicted in the Introduction and the left-hand triangle of Figure 10) has long been overshadowed by the environment.

Unfortunately, it is not nearly as clean as Figure 10 depicts. *The line between what is an environmental issue and what is a social issue is often blurry.* As a result, tradeoffs must often be considered. Availability of fresh water may be seen primarily as an environmental issue in the suburbs of Los Angeles, while it is considered a social issue in the 37 countries that the World Resources Institute rates 4.01 or higher on a 1-to-5 scale of water-stressed countries.

Figure 10: The Changing Sustainability Conversation

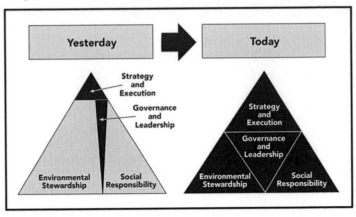

Source: HEDSTROM

The emerging social responsibility agenda is vast and complex. To name a few, the issues of social injustice, economic inequality, and the impacts of digital transformation place social issues squarely in the C-Suite. CEOs are learning the importance of speaking out on topics of critical interest to their employees, as several CEOs did in the aftermath of the Charlottesville, Virginia, uprising in August 2017.

The Opportunity: Glass Half Full

The exploding middle class globally and all that it represents is at the core of significant business opportunities over the next decade – and beyond. Every company, even those sourcing from and selling to suppliers and customers locally in the U.S. or Canada (where populations are fairly stable and the environment is clean) ignores these changes at its peril.

Scenario #1 is the "glass half empty." From a societal point of view, the addition of 2.5 billion consumers represents a massive threat in one sense. With society bumping up against ecosystem limits today (fresh water availability, atmospheric carbon, etc.), future regional wars will be fought over water rights, agricultural land, mineral rights, and the like. (At a local level, wars have been fought over such limits for generations.) In addition, populations are migrating to cities, most of which are already full of smog, vehicles, and congestion.

Climate change is a threat multiplier: it contributes to economic and political instability and also worsens the effects. Climate displacement is becoming one of the world's most powerful and destabilizing geopolitical forces. While data on climate refugees is sparse, in a 2010 Gallup World Poll, respondents representing 500 million adults (roughly one of every fourteen people on the planet) said *severe environmental problems would require them to move within the next five years.*[22] In this (depressing) scenario, the growth industries might be bombs, guns, caskets, pollution controls, border controls, and private police forces.

Scenario #2 is the "glass half full." Doubling the number of people globally represents massive growth markets: in renewable energy; in transportation (sustainable mobility, ride sharing, tomorrow's car-sharing); in food (grown without use of hydrocarbon-based fertilizers and pesticides – and without depleting aquifers); in housing (zero energy, zero impact urban housing, etc.); in affordable health care (access to medicines, water, and food); and in consumer products. Clearly, providing products, services, and solutions to meet these future needs will not be the same as today. *The future simply cannot look like it does today.* Realistically, one cannot even envision a world with twice the number that we have today of cars in cities, big-box stores in suburbia, and CO_2-spewing power plants – and much, much more.

Undoubtedly, both scenarios will play out in various ways, in different sectors and parts of the world, and in pockets of time. Yet **the common thread through both scenarios is *making a business out of solving the world's most pressing challenges.*** As the world becomes more volatile, boards and C-suite executives must make their companies more agile to deal with the increasing disruptive developments.

That will require thinking about solutions in very different ways than companies have been thinking over the past few decades. Moreover, data suggests that *the next generations of consumers, entrepreneurs, and business leaders are ready to pitch in and do their part to solve the world's pressing challenges.* (See Table 6.)

Table 6: Next Generations of Consumers, Entrepreneurs and Business Leaders

Responses by age to the question: *"We should do what is right for the planet, even if it harms the U.S. economy."*		
Generation Descriptor	**Born**	
Matures	Before 1946	48%
Boomers	1946-1964	53%
Xers	1965-1978	62%
Millennials	1979 – 1996	72%
Centennials	After 1997	74%

Source: 2016 US Yankelovich MONITOR

Social Responsibility at a Glance: Tomorrow's Leaders Today

The vast majority of companies that might be considered "leading" today tend to have Stage 3 or Stage 4 practice(s) in one or a few dimensions of social responsibility. One company may be a leader on diversity, another company on supply chain monitoring and verification, and another on community volunteerism. In some cases, the leading initiative is tied directly to a particular passion of the CEO. In other cases (such as *Johnson & Johnson*), leadership is anchored in the company's heritage and core values.

Part One reviewed the critical components of a robust sustainability governance system; *Part Two* addressed how sustainability is factored into corporate strategy and execution; and *Part Three* addressed environmental stewardship. *Part Four* addresses the three "spheres of influence" that characterize social responsibility issues. (See Figure 11.) Below is a brief snapshot of how a few leading companies are addressing these three key areas of social responsibility –

- **Workplace:** Stage 3 companies have a ***workplace environment and supportive core programs that make the company a "great place" to work.*** They set an inclusive and supportive culture at the top (*Cisco, Google, Kimberly-Clark,* and *SAS*); have highly diverse leadership (*Kaiser Permanente, PwC,* and *Sodexo*); have great benefits (*Adobe, Facebook,* and *Salesforce.com*); have outstanding safety culture and performance (*Alcoa* and *DuPont*); or have leading health and wellness programs (*Goldman Sachs, Intuit,* and *Sprint*). Leaders invest in personalized training and staff development related to sustainability.

- **Social Supply Chain:** Stage 3 companies *actively drive social responsibility culture and initiatives throughout their supply chain.* They set high standards and work closely with suppliers to create open and trusted collaboration (*ASML Holding NV* and *Nike) and* incorporate this philosophy into their procurement practices (*Baxter* and *Siemens*). Many leaders today have established a comprehensive supplier sustainability performance measurement system (*Kaiser Permanente* and *Walmart*) and provide strong independent oversight, assurance, and verification of performance (*HP, Intel,* and *Siemens*). Importantly, Stage 3 companies are boldly out in front of their peers on the most material social impact issue in their value chain, as seen by: *Nike* (human rights), *Unilever* and *REI* (labor relations), and *Patagonia* and *Cisco* (child and forced labor).

- **Community:** Stage 3 companies *take philanthropy to a new level as they rethink their company relationship to the global community and the local communities where they operate.* Leading companies focus squarely on initiatives that will help attract tomorrow's best and brightest employees, who will help them produce outstanding competitive advantage. *Intel*'s annual Science Talent Search has a global and inspiring reach. *Danske Bank* (Denmark) helps the growing population of elderly citizens bridge the "digital divide." *IBM* developed an app to allow students to catalogue rainforest biodiversity – a program that squarely addresses both the environmental and social "legs" of sustainability. *JPMorgan Chase* exceeded its initial $100 million investment in the city of Detroit in just three years and now expects to invest $150 million by

2019. The company's goal is to prove the concept: *As more people move up the economic ladder they share in the rewards of a growing economy.*

Figure 11: Social Spheres of Influence

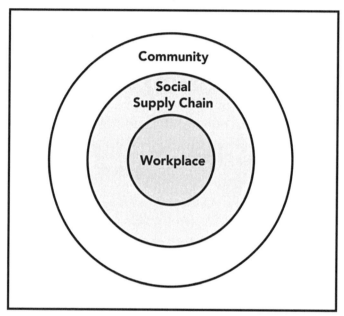

Key Sustainability Indicators: Social Responsibility

Table 7 provides a listing of the rating criteria (Key Sustainability Indicators) associated with Part 4 of the Corporate Sustainability Scorecard: Social Responsibility.

Table 7: Rating Criteria for Social Responsibility

Own Operations: Workplace
General Workplace Environment   • Company's Philosophy re "Workplace"   • Workplace Environment   • Diversity & Inclusion   *Core Workplace Programs*   • Role of Sustainability in Recruitment & Retention   • Linkage of Sustainability to Compensation & Benefits   • Safety Programs & Performance   • Health & Wellness Programs   *Sustainability Capability-Building Initiatives*   • Sustainability Training & Staff Development   • Employee Engagement with Sustainability
Supply Chain – Social Impacts
Posture and Management Processes   • Sustainability Philosophy re Supply Chain   • Supply Chain Risk Assessment & Management   • Responsible Sourcing   • Supply Chain Auditing & Assurance   *Material Supply Chain Impacts*   • Human Rights – including Indigenous People   • Labor Relations/Labor Issues   • Animal Rights   *Supply Chain Partnerships*   • Supplier Capability Building

Table 7 continued : Rating Criteria for Social Responsibility

Community Investment
Community Policies and Programs • Company's Philosophy re "Community" • Philosophy re Community Investment • Philanthropy *Community Investments* • Community Partnerships • Employee Volunteerism in Communities • Community Infrastructure Development *Benefit to Society* • Community Education / Sustainability Learning • Community Job Creation • Community Revitalization

Conclusion

"Business as usual" continues to change dramatically. Today, we stand at a massive, unpredictable, confounding, and seemingly incredulous moment in history. Regardless of industry sector, every traditional company must engage in some soul-searching and in fundamental business transformation in order to survive and thrive.

The ultimate goal today for any company that aims to win in the marketplace is to *decouple growth and profitability from resource intensity*. This challenge brings a whole new definition to being "fit and trim" as a company. It is brutally difficult to achieve these goals: essentially requiring each company to "turn on its head" the basic manufacturing philosophy of the past 150 years. Robust governance is essential.

The *Future-Fit Business Benchmark*[23] embraces the idea of "corporate fitness" as the 21st century unfolds. In the *Corporate Sustainability Scorecard*, Hedstrom Associates approaches corporate fitness from our experience in the boardroom. The Scorecard is built around 17 elements often discussed in board meetings. The Scorecard operationalizes fitness with concrete descriptors of ~150 key sustainability indicators and several hundred selected best-practice company examples of what a Stage 3 or Stage 4 practice looks like today.

Gaining Circular Competitive Advantage

The circular economy may be the biggest revolution in the global economy in 250 years.[24] C-suite executives should be asking themselves: *How do we do this? Where do we start? How do we get the timing right? Is there a logical pathway?*

In order to gain competitive advantage in the emerging circular economy, the C-suite will embrace sustainability in five core ways. Their action list looks like this:

1. **Closed-Loop Supply.** Take an inventory of every material coming into your factory gate. *Put the materials in one of two buckets*: those produced through natural systems and those that are human-made –

   - Natural materials (e.g., agricultural, forest, and fisheries products) should be in a circular loop, such as composting all food and fiber and natural materials.
   - Human-made materials (e.g., metal, plastic, etc.), wherever possible, should be sourced from renewable materials – and recycled forever.

   New and old companies do this today. *Microsoft's* global operations have been 100 percent carbon neutral since 2012. *UPS* offers carbon neutral shipping. *Novelis* is rapidly moving from sourcing 30 percent of its raw material from recycled stock to 80 percent. *Dell* launched carbon negative packaging. Today, *Ecovative, Google,* and *IKEA* invest in renewable energy sourcing on a major scale. *DSM*, the major Dutch chemical company, produces biofuels and bio-based materials made from cellulosic biomass. *Croda* and *Hershey* have achieved 100 percent sustainably sourced palm oil. *Curtis Packaging*, a family-held paper and packaging company, has sourced 100 percent of its energy from renewable sources for years.

2. **Zero Waste.** Once inside the factory gate, place a "wall" around your company's own operations – the things you control. Determine how to drive toward zero waste. This should be the easy part. Almost every company has 20-30 years of experience driving down waste under the "quality" (Lean or Six Sigma) banner. *3M* has worked for 50 years at cutting waste through its Pollution Prevention Pays program. *DuPont* and others followed suit with zero waste ambitions and initiatives. *P&G* and *Subaru* are among the leaders in their industries. Moving toward zero waste employs the same thinking as Lean or Six Sigma. However, "zero waste" thinking is applied on a broader scale, such as in these examples: *Nike* with its Flyknit technology that redefines performance-engineered footwear, and *Reebok* is launching a 100 percent compostable sneaker. Carpetmakers *Shaw Industries* and *Desso* have changed the industry: Shaw Industries launched EcoWorx, a "PVC-free, cradle to cradle certified backing system." Desso's innovative separation technique (Refinity) enables the company to separate the yarn and fibers from the backing – thus greatly enhancing recycling.

3. **Product to Service.** Shifting from selling products to selling services and solutions is nothing new. In the early 1990s, *Xerox* taught us about *leasing* instead of *selling* copy machines; and the company committed to a vision of "*zero waste products from zero waste factories.*" Xerox was definitely ahead of its time. Such approaches are starting to expand. Though *Michelin* is in the business of selling tires, the company has come to realize that customers want *safety* and *mileage*, not just tires. So Michelin is reinventing itself to sell

"mileage" instead of rubber; that is, selling a service rather than a product. Increasingly, customers are driving this shift from product to service. In a recent Conference Board survey, 36 percent of respondents agree that, compared to three years ago, their companies are more likely to use a pay-per-use service of a product instead of buying the product themselves.[25]

4. **Durability.** Companies are looking to extend the durability of products that may not lend themselves to be sold as a service. This is difficult because we have been living in a disposable society for 50+ years (especially in the U.S.). Many businesses have been incented to sell stuff that people use for a while and then throw away. However, future business opportunities lie in finding ways to extend product durability.[26] *Autodesk* teaches sustainability workshops on improving product durability. *DuPont's* weathering systems are certified for product durability. *Caterpillar* products are designed to support "...durability that allows for multiple rebuilds, ease of serviceability and reparability...," while *John Deere's* new L-Series Skidders deliver "best-in-class horsepower as well as improved stability and durability." *Cisco's* VX Tactical, for example, "designed for portability and ease of use in the field is a high-definition video collaboration system with functions that facilitate remote communication and collaboration in remote environments...providing portability, durability, and other functions."

5. **Waste Recovery.** *Waste Management* was forced to reinvent itself when it realized its customers wanted to

create less waste (not more waste). So it flipped its business on its head and determined how to grow the company's revenue by helping its customers generate *less waste* – and how to become smarter about the waste they did generate. This represented a 180-degree shift from the company's history of growing sales by growing the volume of waste coming into its treatment, storage, and disposal system. UK apparel company *H&M* is one of the "biggest users of recycled polyester in the world" noting that one-third of the clothing in the UK goes to landfill. In 2015, 31 of 33 of the *Kroger's* manufacturing plants were designated as "zero waste" facilities.

These five core attributes of gaining circular competitive advantage align with the global shift toward the *"sharing economy."* Sometimes referred to as the peer-to-peer or collaborative economy, the sharing economy is a socio-economic system built around the sharing of human and physical resources. While many sharing economy companies may not place sustainability at the core of their mission, these companies are, in fact, accelerating the sustainability transformation.

Climate Change: The Defining Issue of Our Time

As noted in the Introduction, climate change is, in many ways, the defining issue of the early 21st century. In the Introduction, we noted this –

The "right" conversation about sustainability focuses on corporate positioning and strategy. It begins with a deep examination of the megatrends impacting every company. As reported by the World Economic Forum in its annual (2017) update,[27] *a number of the highest risk megatrends are not only sustainability related but also focused squarely on climate change.* Four of the top five risks are: extreme weather events, failure of climate change mitigation and adaptation, water crises, and large-scale involuntary migration. These risks – interwoven with other societal challenges (e.g., inequality, technology impact of digital transformation on job creation, etc.) – will impact different industry sectors in different ways.

Climate change is a threat multiplier: it contributes to economic and political instability and also worsens the effects. Climate displacement is becoming one of the world's most powerful and destabilizing geopolitical forces. Given this backdrop, it is instructive to look at how the U.S. Navy has been – and is currently – responding to climate change. This is especially timely given the Trump Administration's position on climate change (withdrawing the U.S. from the Paris Agreement), as well as the growing conversation about the subject across the United States. According to a March 2017 Gallup poll, 45 percent of Americans worry "a great deal" about global warming, up from 37 percent in 2016 and 32 percent in 2015.[28] That was before record heat in California, wild fires in the west, and three major hurricanes: Harvey (Houston), Irma (Florida) and Maria (Puerto Rico).

Thirty years ago, the two core responses to climate change – mitigation and adaptation – could be considered interchangeable. As the *Harvard Business Review* reported in its 2017 article about the U.S. Navy: that window has shut.[29] The Navy has very strong *mitigation* efforts under way to reduce its massive footprint with a goal of sourcing 50 percent of its energy from renewable sources by 2020. Yet, the vast majority of the Navy's efforts are around *adaptation* to climate change. The Navy understands that climate change is triggering international conflict, state failure, more prolonged droughts, and wars over water. They see the Arctic opening and realize that the Navy lacks the assets it needs to operate effectively in that region.

In the same way that the U.S. Navy is mitigating its impacts and adapting to the future realities that are ever-present today, each company needs to *be resilient* and *prepare for disruptions*. Mass migrations, climate disruptions, and relocations are happening today. This adaptation often means operating outside of your comfort zone.

Resilient: Capacity to Innovate Amidst Disruptions

Perhaps more than any other trait, the "need to operate outside of its comfort zone" will characterize tomorrow's elite corporation. Why? At its core, sustainability is about not only being fit and trim, but also *resilient*.

Companies must build the capacity to adapt and innovate amidst disruptions. They need to adopt and embrace what can be an uncomfortable set of assumptions about the world around us. Sustainability requires: (1) "unlearning" how industrial society has operated for 150 years, and (2) "charting a new route" to reach the same goal of delivering shareholder value.

Going forward, C-suite executives and boards must treat social responsibility and environmental stewardship not as separate functions largely disconnected from strategy, but rather as integral to corporate and business strategy. This requires CEOs and those who succeed them to be better prepared to make decisions about the environmental and societal impacts of sustainability – and the important tradeoffs required. Likewise, the connection between public policy and strategy is becoming interwoven. The power of social media magnifies the risk of stumbling on a key social or environmental issue of keen interest to employees, customers, or other stakeholders.

The Path Forward

Sometimes individuals, companies, and countries make things too complicated. It is true that sustainability can be complex, challenging, perplexing, and amorphous. The objectives for sustainability include everything from solving climate change and tackling world hunger to protecting human rights and providing access to potable water.

Yet, tomorrow's leading companies systematically will shed their old ways of doing business in the "take-make-waste" world. With a new understanding, they will embrace, drive, and reap the benefits from the circular economy, where business activity is reconsidered as a closed-loop instead of a chain.[30] As noted in the Introduction, *the resource revolution represents the biggest business opportunity in a century.* McKinsey notes that rather than settling for historic resource-productivity improvement rates of one to two percentage points a year, companies need to deliver productivity gains of 50 percent or so every few years.[31] Incremental improvement such as energy efficiency gains of two to three percent per year will no longer cut it.

At its core, *sustainability is about leadership*. Sadly, for the past 20 years, we have had a collective failure of leadership – across government, industry, and civil society. The vast majority of companies over the past two decades have more or less continued "business as usual." Few have taken bold measures. They go on with their day-to-day business in designing, making, and selling the same stuff as in the past. They know sustainability is important. They assign a senior executive to look after it. They set goals and reduce their footprints. They report progress and try to be more transparent. Yet, honestly, the majority of companies today continue to *dabble* in sustainability. They see ESG issues almost entirely as risks to manage. Moreover, many C-suite executives have yet to view the "power of sustainability" to drive profitable growth and value creation.

The Corporate Sustainability Scorecard C-suite rating system comes in here. Aimed specifically at the C-suite and the board (perhaps via those advising them), the Scorecard can help create the right conversations about both governance and leadership, and strategy and execution.

At some point...

...the first light bulb goes on in the C-suite or boardroom. Board members "see" the mess that humans are making of the planet and the coming global impact of doubling middle-class consumption on this planet with fixed resources. They think about stranded assets; and they recognize that sustainability risks and opportunities are several orders of magnitude higher than in the past...

...and then a second light bulb goes on. The executive team begins to see the massive growth of the global middle class not only as a source of risk, but also as a huge business opportunity. They imagine growing a profitable business without consuming non-renewable resources.

Today's leading companies are positioning themselves to grow and profit from addressing the world's most pressing challenges. As companies transform and realign toward this new overarching goal, *sustainability leadership* in the C-suite and boardroom can be enabled by this simple agenda –

- Anticipate trends.
- Understand new and diverse risks.
- Determine what it would take to be carbon neutral.
- Target zero waste throughout the value chain.
- Work with your suppliers and customers to "close the loop" on everything.
- Understand the agendas of people who can influence your business.
- Inspire your employees.
- Prevent nasty surprises.
- Be proud to tell your kids what you do.

The leaders of today's companies have a choice: *Will we transform with the times and position our company as a fit, trim, and resilient company of tomorrow? Or will we "stay the course" and hope for the best?*

Game on!

Appendix A: Definitions

Definitions
• **Assurance Letter**: Typically an annual signed statement from business executives (often business presidents) to the CEO stating that operations are in compliance; risks and significant issues are identified and being managed; and processes are in place to ensure consistent implementation of corporate policies and values.
• **Chief Sustainability Officer (CSO)**: The most senior person in the company with responsibility for overseeing sustainability policy, positioning and activities.
• **Circular Economy**: An alternative to the traditional linear economy (make, use, dispose) in which resources remain in use for as long as possible, extracting the maximum value from them while in use, then recover and regenerate products and materials at the end of each product or service life.
• **Closed-Loop**: Similar to the circular economy, in closed-loop recycling, materials (at the end of their useful life) are consistently repurposed, recycled, reused, reclaimed, restored, or otherwise converted to some use rather than discharged as waste.
• **ESG (Environment, Social, Governance)**: The term often used by the investment community to refer to what they characterize as the three central factors in measuring the "sustainability" of an investment in a company or business. In this book and the companion website, the term ESG is used interchangeably with sustainability.

Definitions
• **Executive Sustainability Council**: The senior-level, cross-functional group of executives that many companies have to provide a forum for setting policy direction; recommending goals and metrics; deciding priorities; allocating resources; and reviewing progress on key initiatives.
• **External Sustainability Advisory Board**: A group of sustainability experts or thought leaders from various external stakeholder groups, assembled to periodically advise the CEO, executive team and board of directors.
• **Externality**: The cost or benefit that affects a party who did not choose to incur that cost or benefit. For example, manufacturing activities that cause air pollution or carbon emissions may impose health, cleanup, or other costs on society.
• **Footprint**: A measure of an organization's (or human's) demand on the Earth's ecosystems. In the sustainability context, "footprint" is used as a measure of the full environmental and social impacts across the supply chain of an organization's operations, including, for example, consumption, use and emissions of energy, materials, resources, water, etc.
• **Global Reporting Initiative (GRI)**: A non-profit organization that produces one of the world's most prevalent standards for sustainability reporting.
• **International Sustainability Charters/Commitments**: A global sustainability charter, framework or set of principles such as, for example, the UN Global Compact; UN Declaration on Human Rights; the Precautionary Principle; Green Chemistry Principles; etc. Also includes commitments to global agreements such as the Paris Climate Accord.

Definitions
• **Key Business Decisions**: The handful of major decisions the CEO and Board make each year – typically involving merger, acquisition or divestiture; large capital expenditure; new product launch; major research and development expenditure, etc.
• **Key Sustainability Indicators (KSI)**: Hedstrom Associates uses the term "Key Sustainability Indicators" to define the rating criteria in our Corporate Sustainability Scorecard C-suite rating system. The Corporate Sustainability Scorecard allows a user to rate a company on about 150 Key Sustainability Indicators.
• **Life-Cycle Assessment (LCA)**: A technique to assess environmental impacts associated with all the stages of a product's life from-cradle-to-grave (i.e., from raw material extraction through materials processing, manufacture, distribution, use, repair and maintenance, and disposal or recycling). Also known as life-cycle analysis.
• **Material**: Information is material if its omission or misstatement could influence the economic decision of users taken on the basis of the financial statements.
• **Materiality**: A concept or convention within the financial community relating to the importance/significance of something relevant to the corporation. Information is material if its omission or misstatement could influence the economic decision of users taken on the basis of the financial statements. Materiality in relation to the inclusion of information in an integrated (financial and sustainability) report refers to matters that "could substantively affect the organization's ability to create value over the short, medium and long term."[32]
• **Non-Governmental Organization (NGO)**: An organization that is neither a part of a government nor a conventional for-profit business; seen to represent "civil society."

Definitions

- **Product, Service, or Solution (PSS)**: Items or services sold by companies that are intended to satisfy a market need. From a sustainability context, shifting from selling products to leasing products or selling services is consistent with moving from a linear ("take – make – waste") system to a closed-loop one whereby products, after their useful life, are recycled, reused, refurbished, or returned to some productive use.

- **Sharing Economy**: While there is not one widely agreed definition, the sharing economy involves attempts to make more efficient use of labor and capital resources through the use of information technology that lowers the costs of matching buyer with sellers.

- **Stakeholder**: Individuals or groups of people who can reasonably be expected to be significantly affected by an organization's business activities, outputs or outcomes, or whose actions can reasonably be expected to significantly affect the ability of the organization to create value over time.
  - "Internal stakeholders" typically include the organization's governing body, management, employees and shareholders.
  - "External stakeholders" typically include communities, government, environmental groups, as well as suppliers, customers and consumers.

- **Sustainable Development Goals (SDGs)**: A set of 17 "Global Goals" with 169 targets, adopted by 193 member countries of the United Nations, intended to galvanize and guide the world's efforts to eradicate poverty, end hunger and address climate change by 2030.

Definitions
• **Sustainability**: The pursuit of a business growth strategy that creates long-term shareholder value by seizing opportunities and managing risks related to the company's environmental and social impacts. Sustainability includes conventional environment, health and safety (EHS) management; community involvement and philanthropy; labor and workplace conditions as well as elements of corporate citizenship, corporate governance, supply chain and procurement.
• **Sustainability Principles**: Various ways of characterizing the concept of sustainability. One example would be the four system conditions of The Natural Step.
• **Sustainability Report**: An organizational report that gives information about ESG positioning and performance. This can be a stand-alone report (often a companion to the Annual Report); it can be included with the financial information in a fully "integrated report;" or can be the equivalent information available on a company's website.
• **Unwritten Rules of the Game**: how a cross-section of employees would describe "the way things work around here."

Appendix B: Scorecard Elements

Governance and Leadership
1. **Vision, Mission, Values**: The *public statements* articulating a company's *raison d'être* (reason for existing); the less formal but critically important *private actions* a company takes to reinforce its values, mission, and vision; and the *external recognition* received from credible organizations.
2. **CEO Leadership**: The way in which the CEO *manages his/her own agenda* to drive sustainability throughout the company; *manages the Board of Directors agenda*; and *structures the sustainability organization and initiatives* within the company.
3. **Board of Directors Leadership**: The *structure and resources* of the board committee(s) providing oversight of sustainability; the *assurance processes* that report on sustainability risks and opportunities to the Board; and the *Board's commitment of time* to learning about sustainability issues, best practices, and trends.
4. **Goals and Metrics**: The overall approach to establishing and tracking performance against sustainability goals, including the *goal-setting process*; the *time horizon* for framing the goals and metrics; and the *content and impact* of the individual targets that are set, measured, and reported on.
5. **Culture and Organization**: The *management attention and accountability* directed to sustainability by the CEO and executive team; the *key culture indicators related to sustainability* in place that define the actual culture (including the "unwritten rules of the game"); and the *sustainability organization* (structure and people) leading the charge.

6.	**Stakeholder Engagement**: The quality and impact of engaging with external stakeholders on sustainability: *why they engage*; *who they engage with*; *what issues they engage on*; and *how and when they engage.*
7.	**Disclosure, Reporting and Transparency**: The information that is *disclosed* to stakeholders related to own operations, suppliers, and the full supply chain sustainability impacts; the way in which sustainability data and information is *reported*; and the extent to which the company has earned a reputation for *transparency.*

Strategy and Execution

8.	**Strategic Planning**: The *business drivers* that frame how the CEO and CFO think about sustainability; the strategy; the operational and capital *planning processes*; and the *output* of how environmental / societal risks and opportunities are incorporated into plans, personal objectives, and budgets.
9.	**Innovation, Research and Development**: The *role innovation plays* in the business and the extent to which sustainability is connected to innovation; the *processes and methodologies* for embedding sustainability into innovation, research, and development; and the *output* of innovation investments.
10.	**Customers and Markets**: The *core approach* a company takes to address customer needs; the *sustainability linkage to customers*; and the role sustainability plays in *shaping future market opportunities* the company is pursuing.
11.	**Products, Services and Solutions:** The *fundamental product positioning* of the company; the extent to which sustainability principles are incorporated formally into *existing products, services, and solutions;* and the role sustainability plays in driving *future products, services, and solutions* to drive top-line revenue growth.

Environmental Stewardship
12. **Environmental Footprint – Operations**: Environmental impacts associated with wholly owned or partially owned operations, including *managing purchased resource inputs, managing own physical footprint,* and *managing non-product outputs* (emissions and wastes).
13. **Supply Chain Environmental Impacts**: Managing the environmental impacts of the company's supply chain, including the *posture and management processes* governing supplier interactions; the means of *addressing the most material supplier impacts*; and the *nature and extent of supplier sustainability partnerships.*
14. **Environmental Footprint – Products**: Managing the environmental impacts of the company's products, including the *overall product stewardship approach,* the *product design process,* and *end-of-life product management* following retail, consumer use, and disposal.
Social Responsibility
15. **Own Operations: Workplace:** The *general workplace environment* established by management and seen by the employees; the *core workplace programs* to promote safety, health, and employee wellbeing; and the *sustainability capability-building initiatives* in place.
16. **Supply Chain Social Impacts:** The *philosophy and policy regarding human capital* implemented by the company across its supply chain; the *processes and programs* in place to build human capital by investing in employees, contractors, and the broader workforce; and the *supply chain social initiatives* under way.
17. **Community Investment:** The company's *community policies and programs*; the *community investments* made by the company; and the *benefits to society* from those initiatives and investments.

Appendix C: About the Sustainability Scorecard

The Corporate Sustainability Scorecard™ C-suite rating system is designed for use by corporations – especially large corporations. (Visit: www.thesustainabilityscorecard.com.)

Though the Scorecard can be used by various individuals and groups within a company, the tool is designed primarily for use by (and discussions with) the executive team. Typically, use of the Scorecard is led by the officer who oversees internal sustainability efforts and reports to the CEO and Board of Directors (or Board Committee) about sustainability posture, programs, performance, and plans. For sustainability officers, the Scorecard places the entire sustainability conversation in a simple board-friendly context.

Corporate executives use the Scorecard to map their company's current position on a one-to-four maturity scale so that they can know with confidence:

- Where their company stacks up vis-à-vis sustainability (in other words, where they are on the maturity path);

- How their company compares with competitors and peers; and

- What "best practice" (defined as a Stage 3 or Stage 4 practice) looks like today.

The Scorecard's summary table (depicted in Figure 4) is supported by a robust methodology. It is organized into –

- *Four parts.* The four main sections of the Sustainability Scorecard include: *Governance and Leadership, Strategy and Execution, Environmental Stewardship,* and *Social Responsibility.*

- *Seventeen elements*. Within the four parts described above, 17 topics (elements) comprise the overall Corporate Sustainability Scorecard. Each element (e.g., "CEO Leadership") is defined briefly or characterized in Appendix B.

- *~150 Key Sustainability Indicators.* For each of the 17 elements of the Scorecard, executives rate the company on 8 to 12 "sub-elements" that we call "Key Sustainability Indicators." (Note: the current version of the Scorecard has 157 Key Sustainability Indicators. The precise number may vary slightly over time based on feedback from registered users of the Scorecard.)

- *~600 Descriptors.* Text is provided in the individual rating columns (Stage 1, Stage 2, etc., on each Scorecard Template).

Individuals can gain access to the online rating tool by visiting the website and reviewing the various "Join" options. Individuals who meet the join criteria become a "registered user" and receive a username and password, providing access to the "back end" of the website with the full rating system.

Additionally, registered users can purchase the *Handbook for The Corporate Sustainability Scorecard*, a companion guide to the online rating system. The *Handbook* includes detailed rating templates for each element of the Scorecard (all ~600 descriptors for the ~150 Key Sustainability Indicators). These are the same rating criteria used to create a company self-assessment on the website. The *Handbook* also includes the over 200 corporate "best practice" case examples found on the website.

The Scorecard is designed not only as a tool, but also as a collaborative learning process. Companies have successfully used it in a facilitated meeting of the C-suite, Board, or a senior cross-functional team. Having identified very clearly how their company "stacks up" today, C-suite executives use the Scorecard to engage in a typically deep and profound discussion of how they want to position the company for future growth – leveraging the mega-trends impacting society.

A final point: While the Hedstrom Associates team does not expect the fundamental structure of the Scorecard to change, we do anticipate that over time the individual Key Sustainability Indicators – and the descriptors of those KSI's for Stages 1-4 – will evolve. Moreover, we expect the hundreds of best practice company examples to change on a continuing basis. Users are encouraged to submit their own suggestions of a Stage 3 or Stage 4 practice (of their own company or of a company they admire). The Hedstrom Associates team will continue to update the scorecard templates and best practice examples periodically and to provide those to individuals who subscribe to (and are provided full access to the rating templates on) www.TheSustainabilityScorecard.com.

Acknowledgments

The *Corporate Sustainability Scorecard* C-suite rating system has been influenced and shaped profoundly by conversations I have had in corporate boardrooms. In 1997, two of the Fortune 500 corporate Board of Directors meetings I participated in sowed the seeds for the Scorecard. In both meetings, the committee members discussed sustainability, while groping for a tool that could help them get their arms around the issues. That was when I started crafting the Corporate Sustainability Scorecard.

To the long-standing clients who engaged me to work on their behalf, and who entrusted me to meet with their CEOs and present to their boards of directors, I am most grateful. Since 1997, I have had the privilege of working with hundreds of outstanding leaders in large corporations across the globe – at the intersection of business strategy, corporate governance, and sustainability. You have challenged my assumptions, shaped my thinking, and helped create the robust content of the Scorecard. Thank you!

In 2015, twenty-five companies participated in a pilot initiative of the web-based Scorecard. You worked through the Scorecard; participated in webinars; and provided feedback. The contributions from that pilot helped simplify and sharpen the rating tool, updated on the website (www.thesustainabilityscorecard.com).

Many of the companies involved in the 2015 pilot are members of The Conference Board's various sustainability councils where I serve as Program Director. The

Conference Board has been a strong partner in advancing the business and sustainability agenda over the past two decades. In 2015, they published my article, *"Navigating the Sustainability Transformation,"* essentially an early version of this book's Introduction. A special "thank you" to Conference Board colleagues Thomas Singer, Jim Hendricks, and Uwe Schulte for your constructive partnership.

A core team of Hedstrom Associates colleagues (Beth Tener, Pat Mahon, Justine Pattantyus, Larry Krupp, Nick Braica, and Kelsa Summer) has been with me over the past decade, working to create this Scorecard. Your patience and always positive support has kept the Scorecard moving. And I extend a special "thank you" to my colleagues from earlier days at consulting firm Arthur D. Little, especially those with whom I worked closely in Europe for many years: Jonathan Shopley, Richard Clarke, Rick Eagar, and their teams who helped shape the early versions of the Scorecard.

Many colleagues have read and commented on versions of the Scorecard and this book, including Stephanie Aument, Bill Blackburn, Jim Hamilton, Stuart Hart, Andy Hoffman, Jason Jay, Alex Lajoux, Julie O'Brien, Dawn Rittenhouse, Gwen Ruta, Larry Selzer, Karl Schmidt, Dave Stangis, Ken Tierney, Bob Willard, and Terry Yosie. Thank you! Your insights and broad perspective continue to amaze me.

Finally, nothing has shaped my thinking about this Scorecard more than the time I have spent in highly confidential sessions with corporate board members, one of whom stands out. To my long-time friend and mentor, Patrick F. Noonan, my heartfelt thanks.

About the Author

Gilbert (Gib) Hedstrom has over 30 years of experience advising CEOs and board members about how to handle difficult environmental and business challenges. After 20 years at consulting firm Arthur D. Little, where he was Vice President and Managing Director, Gib launched Hedstrom Associates in 2004. Gib provides consulting services to companies about issues that lie at the intersection of corporate governance, strategy, and sustainability.

Gib has reported to full boards of directors or board committees (with oversight of corporate responsibility issues) of major global corporations on over 60 occasions. In his role as independent sustainability advisor, he counsels directors concerning the risks and opportunities, and shares examples of "best practices" globally. He often meets with outside directors in "executive session" (without members of management present).

His clients have included Accenture, AES, Air Products, Alcoa, Ashland, Autodesk, Bayer, Baxter, Boeing, BP, Calvert, Coca-Cola, Conoco, Cytec, Dell, Ford, HP, Honeywell, Kodak, Monsanto, Novartis, Novo Nordisk, Pemex, Raytheon, Sask Power, Shell, Tyco, United Technologies, USG, and United States Steel, among many others.

For The Conference Board, Gib serves as Program Director of *Sustainability Council I: Strategy and Implementation, Sustainability Council II: Innovation and Growth,* and the *Chief Environment, Health, and Safety Officers' Council.* These councils provide the opportunity to interact constantly with executives of about 100 leading companies

– and to keep his finger on the pulse of the current challenges.

Gib has authored several books and written dozens of articles related to the environment, governance, strategy, and sustainability. Frequently, he is called upon to speak on business risks and opportunities created by environmental and social trends.

Gib has dual master's degrees from the University of Michigan (MBA Corporate Strategy; MS Natural Resource Management) and a BA (Economics and Geology) from Hamilton College. He welcomes further discussion about governance, strategy, and sustainability issues, and can be reached at gib@hedstromassociates.com.

Notes

[1] Homi Charas, "The Unprecedented Expansion of the Global Middle Class: an Update," Brookings, February 2017.

[2] "GEO-5 for Business: Impacts of a Changing Environment on the Corporate Sector," United Nations Environment Program's fifth Global Environment Outlook (GEO-5) Report, June 2012.

[3] Gilbert S. Hedstrom, "Navigating the Sustainability Transformation," *Director Notes*, The Conference Board, January 2015.

[4] "Population 2030: Demographic challenges and opportunities for sustainable development planning," United Nations, 2015.

[5] "Geo-5 for Business," *op cit.*

[6] "Embedding a carbon price into business strategy," CDP North America, Inc., September 2016, p. 5.

[7] Stefan Heck and Matt Rogers, "Are you ready for the resource revolution?" *McKinsey Quarterly*, March 2014, p. 2.

[8] "Environmental and Social Proposals in the 2017 Proxy Season," The Conference Board, September 2017.

[9] Gilbert S. Hedstrom, "GEMI Quick Guide: Sustainability 101," Global Environmental Management Initiative, October 2015.

[10] "The Global Risks Report 2017, 12th Edition," World Economic Forum, 2017, p. 4. http://www3.weforum.org/docs/GRR17_Report_web.pdf

[11] http://www.ashland.com/about/ashland-way

[12] "Corporate sustainability: Unilever CEO Paul Polman on ending the "three month rat race," Reuters, October 2012.

[13] "The Seven Pillars of Sustainability Leadership," The Conference Board2016, p. 19.

[14] "2009 NACD Public Company Governance Survey," National Association of Corporate Directors, 2009.

[15] "2016-2017 NACD Public Company Governance Survey," National Association of Corporate Directors, 2016.

[16] "King Report on Governance for South Africa 2009," *King III*, last modified September 7, 2009, p. 11. (http://c.ymcdn.com/sites/www.iodsa.co.za/resource/resmgr/king_iii/King_Report_on_Governance_fo.pdf)

[17] "The Conference Board CEO Challenge 2016," The Conference Board, Research Report 1599, January 2016, P. 67.

[18] Thomas Singer, "Driving Revenue Growth through Sustainable Products and Services," The Conference Board, Research Report 1583, June 2015. (https://www.conference-board.org/webcasts/ondemand/webcastdetail.cfm?webcastid=3473)

[19] Thomas Singer, "Driving Revenue Growth," *op cit.*

[20] "SD-KPI Standard 2016-2021," SD-M GmbH, September 2016.

[21] "SASB Conceptual Framework," Sustainability Accounting Standards Board (SASB), February 2017.

[22] Neli Esipova, Julie Ray, and Anita Pugliese, "The Many Faces of Global Migration," International Organization for Migration, in collaboration with Gallup, 2011.

[23] "Future-Fit Business Benchmark – *Release 1*," May 2016. (http://futurefitbusiness.org)

[24] Peter Lacy, "Gaining an Edge from the Circle: Growth, Innovation and Customer Value through the Circular Economy," *Accenture Strategy*, 2015.

[25] Thomas Singer, "Business Transformation and the Circular Economy, *op cit.*

[26] Thomas Singer, "Business Transformation and the Circular Economy, *op cit.*

[27] "The Global Risks Report 2017, 12th Edition," World Economic Forum, 2017, p. 4. http://www3.weforum.org/docs/GRR17_Report_web.pdf

[28] "Global Warming Concern at Three-Decade High in US," Gallup, March 14, 2017.

[29] Forest L. Reinhardt and Michael W. Toffel, "Managing Climate Change: Lessons from the U.S. Navy," *Harvard Business Review*, July-August 2017, p. 103-111.

[30] Thomas Singer, "Business Transformation and the Circular Economy: A Candid Look at Risks and Rewards," The Conference Board, 2017.

[31] Heck and Rogers, *op cit.*

[32] The International Integrated Reporting Council, The International <IR> Framework (13 December 2013), p. 5. (http://integratedreporting.org/resource/international-ir-framework/)

77789952R00064

Made in the USA
Lexington, KY
02 January 2018